Legacy of
LEADERSHIP

Admiral Lord Nelson

Legacy of
LEADERSHIP

Lessons from Admiral Lord Nelson

Joseph F. Callo

Hellgate Press
Central Point, Oregon

Legacy of Leadership: Lessons from Admiral Lord Nelson

Hellgate Press
a division of PSI Research
P.O. Box 3727
Central Point, OR 97502-0032

(541) 479-9464
(541) 476-1479 *fax*
info@psi-research.com *e-mail*

Edit, book design, and maps: Constance C. Dickinson
Composition: Jan O. Olsson
Cover design: Steven Burns

Callo, Joseph F., 1929–
　　Legacy of leadership : lessons from Admiral Lord Nelson / Joseph F. Callo. — 1st ed.
　　　　p. cm.
　　Includes bibliographical references and index.
　　ISBN 1-55571-510-9
　　　　1. Nelson, Horatio Nelson, Viscount, 1758–1805—Military leadership. 2. Great
Britain—History, Naval—18th century. 3. Admirals—Great Britain—Biography. I. Title.

DA87.1.N4 C25　1999
359'.0092—dc21
　　[B]　　　　　　　　　　　　　　　　　　　　　　　　　　　　　　　　99-047211

Frontispiece. This engraving by A. Carden from an original drawing by H. Edridge as shown in the abridged edition of *The Life of Admiral Lord Nelson, K.B.*, by Reverend James Stanier Clarke and John M'Arthur and published in 1810 by T. Cadell and W. Davies in the Strand, London, is from the author's collection.

Printed and bound in the United States of America
First edition 10 9 8 7 6 5 4 3 2 1

 Printed on recycled paper when available.

To my wife, Sally, and
to my children, Joe, Jim, Mary Ellen, Kat, Trish, and R. J.

Contents

Foreword

In this book Admiral Callo has set sail in the wake of Nelson, pursuing the elusive qualities of leadership that manifest themselves in combat. Few will dispute an assertion that Nelson spawned a personal legacy of success in battle. Callo makes the specific case that Nelson's combat leadership, annealed in time's crucible, is a unique force that reaches across two centuries to inspire today's naval warriors. He also rightly points out the danger of failing to foster leaders who will win in war.

On the one hand, the ships of Nelson's time changed little, and in fact, the quality of his ships was often inferior to that of his opponents. On the other hand, he sailed in ships manned by British tars and led by a group of officers that had no equal. This suggests that a number of Nelson's contemporaries could have led the Royal Navy to pound, punish, and destroy Napoleon's Continental alliance. Not true. Nelson's unique contribution to warfare at sea was in changing how captains and admirals fought their ships. By the time he fought his last battle at Trafalgar, the British tars and Royal Navy officers had no equal, and Britain had no equal on the world's oceans.

The navies of the mid-eighteenth century usually engaged each other in accordance with a rigid set of rules or conventions. These were known as King James Fighting Instructions. The primacy of these instructions in the Royal Navy was reinforced by an infamous court martial, which resulted in the hanging of an admiral who failed to follow them. "To get the attention of the others," it is said. The dominant characteristic of fleet engagements of the time was that the opposing forces would form in columns, maneuver on parallel courses, and trade broadsides. Battles fought in this pre-Nelson style were often inconclusive and favored the status quo. For example, the encounter between the British and French forces of Admirals Hood and DeGrasse at the entrance of Chesapeake Bay—the only fleet action of the American Revolution—was inconclusive. And strategically Hood's failure to brush the French aside sealed the fate of Cornwallis at Yorktown.

The key point is that between the time Nelson first assumed command at sea in 1778, to his death at Trafalgar in 1805, his unique combat leadership drove a change in the basic form of battle. It was not so much that the Royal Navy prevailed but the way they won that was the agent of change and the foundation of the Nelson legacy of leadership.

This book includes five battles to illustrate Nelson's legacy. Each shows that Nelson understood the link between personal combat leadership directed towards victory in a specific battle and the longer-term strategic sea power issues. The battles also illustrate how he worked out ahead of time, not only the tactical options, but also the overall approach—what we know today as combat doctrine. He formed a scheme of battle, inspired his captains to believe that that was the way to win, and trained his ships' crews accordingly. The same principle is electronically incorporated into today's cutting edge Aegis Combat System as an "Auto Special," a predetermined combat doctrine that has already been agreed to by those involved.

Nelson shaped Royal Navy combat doctrine on the anvil of success, and it has lasted for two centuries. Geopolitics, national economics, and weapons systems have changed, but the essentials of Nelson's combat doctrine have remained at the core of the Royal Navy. Doubters of that should study the Falklands War.

For the U.S. Navy, one who stands out as a combat leader in the spiritual line descended from Nelson is Admiral Arleigh "31-knot" Burke. A series of incidents during World War II, when Burke was earning a reputation as a superb destroyer commander and tactician, are instructive.

The events began in March of 1943, when the clouds of the U.S. Navy's heavy loses at Savo Island had not dissipated and the battle for Guadalcanal was still in doubt. Burke was commander of Destroyer Division Forty-five in Kula Gulf when his division engaged a group of Japanese combatants. Burke ordered a salvo of ten torpedoes fired from his flagship. The captain of the ship fired only five torpedoes and all missed. In the after-action evaluation, Burke accepted the fault for the opportunity lost. He concluded that he had failed to insure that he and his captains were of one mind before the action started.

Several months later the key to victory at the battle of Cape St. George was a night torpedo attack, flawlessly executed by his ships. A winning doctrine had emerged from the previous failure. Burke, like Nelson, was not immune from failure. Nelson moved beyond the static battle concepts of his time, and Burke did the same. A critical common denominator, something that had nothing to do with technology, was the establishing of a winning combat doctrine within a fighting force.

This book, focuses on Nelson's life, times, and particularly, his legacy of winning combat leadership. It asks the question: will the warriors of hopefully a very distant day be ready "to answer the bell"—and win—when their time comes? The Navy's record is cause for optimism; Arleigh Burke and his World War II contemporaries are convincing evidence. And perhaps the best answer to the question can be found in the spirit behind Admiral Burke's admonishment to the first crew of his namesake ship, the USS *Arleigh Burke*:

"This ship was built to fight, you had better know how." His emphasis was Nelsonian.

Vice Admiral Joseph Metcalf, III
U.S. Navy, Retired

Editor's Note: Admiral Metcalf is a U.S. Naval Academy graduate whose last assignment before retirement was Deputy Chief of Naval Operations for Surface Warfare. His operational specialty is surface warfare, and he has commanded both ships and fleets in combat. He commanded all U.S. forces during the dramatically successful rescue campaign in Granada. Among the medals worn by Admiral Metcalf are the Distinguished Service Medal with three gold stars, the Defense Superior Service Medal, Legion of Merit with two gold stars, Bronze Star with combat V and gold star, and the Combat Action Ribbon. Currently Admiral Metcalf is an independent consultant on naval affairs.

Chapter 1

Value of a Legacy

Vice Admiral Lord Nelson had an astonishing life. Historians see his exploits as a determining force during the Napoleonic Wars. For navalists his victories of the late eighteenth and early nineteenth centuries are case histories for winning naval tactics in the age of sail. For many others his career in the British Royal Navy was simply so dramatic that it's a highly entertaining sea saga.

Nelson was respected by Napoleon, feared by his adversaries at sea, needed by his seniors in the British government and the Royal Navy, followed into hellish combat by those who served with him, venerated by the public during his career, and loved by his wife and paramour. He was a genuine legend in his own time. Today, however, Nelson's life also provides a unique opportunity to refocus on a particularly timely subject, combat leadership.

We live in an era characterized by built-to-budget military forces and so-called low intensity conflicts married to high intensity politics. Because of the unique pressures of those circumstances, the importance of combat leadership isn't getting the public attention it deserves.[1] As a result we are, as a nation, in danger of compromising a unique national resource and an absolutely essential element of our defense capability: military leaders who will win in combat. In addition, in the present environment of come-as-you-are conflicts, we are not going to have much opportunity to "grow" winning warfighters after a major conflict begins.

One of the additional problems we face in trying to maintain a cadre of winning combat leaders is the current impact of political correctness on military careers. When the careers of proven combat leaders are blasted—not on the basis of professional mistakes or serious misconduct, but on the basis of political incorrectness—the message throughout the military is clear; political skill is the primary requirement for career advancement. When training requirements are "normed" to accommodate gender differences the message again is clear; standards of military performance are less important than social objectives. The result of these lessons is that too many of those with combat leadership potential—from junior, to midgrade, to senior levels—simply get out of the military.

Today that's exactly what is happening, in eye-popping numbers. A writer in a recent article in *The Wall Street Journal* summed it up in very clear terms. He wrote, "The American military culture, established through two centuries of tradition, is under attack like it never has been before. The warrior is being overtaken by the technologist, and in the pursuit of opportunity for all, the fighting elites are now being targeted as no longer relevant to accomplishing the objectives of war."[2] The down-the-road cost of these circumstances—in terms of American lives, core values, and global influence—is yet to be reckoned.

Still another serious problem is the growing lack of military experience among the governmental, educational, and media leaders of the nation. The sinking proportion of members of Congress with significant military service—now reduced to roughly 30 percent—typifies the problem. As a result there is not a wide appreciation of the importance of encouraging those with the potential to lead successfully in combat.

The dangerous tendency to forget the critical need to cultivate potential combat leaders is aggravated, in addition, by today's narrow national defense focus on technology and systems. This concentration on factors other than leadership is, interestingly, common in today's business and professional worlds, as well. However, Nelson's life challenges the technocratic, management-over-leadership approach. In battle he functioned beyond the technology and tactics of his time. And by sheer force of will and personality he, more than any British naval leader of his era, contributed to the establishment of that nation as master of the seas.

In the process of getting beyond the limits of the technology and politics of his time, Nelson overcame the bureaucratic drags of Whitehall and the Admiralty. Despite the separation in time, the bureaucratic obstacles that were faced by Nelson were not unlike the multiple layers of civilian administration weighing down the American military today. He also overcame budget driven defense policies—again not unlike those America is presently facing—to change the course of history from the decks of his ships.

Of particular significance, Nelson achieved his victories at an important juncture of history, a period when the oceans were completing the 400-year transition from barriers to bridges that began in the Age of Discovery. It was a time when the ability to use the seas had matured as a measure of national potential. For Britain this translated to a pursuit of mercantilist policies that were dependent on the use of the oceans for commerce and the projection of military power. In terms of our own time, the end of the twentieth century also appears to be an historical juncture, one defined by a new order of deliverability and lethality in military weapons.

Admittedly much has changed on the geopolitical landscape during the two centuries since Nelson's time. Imperialism and colonialism have waned; Pax Americana has replaced Pax Britannica. To some degree governments that are more representative of the people have replaced absolute rulers. Certainly the faces and locations of America's potential military enemies are very different than those confronting Britain during Nelson's era. And at sea the technology of combat has evolved from wooden square-riggers with solid-shot cannons to a high-tech array of subsurface, surface, air, and, presumably in the future, space weapons systems.

But if there are significant differences between Nelson's times and today, there are also provocative parallels. For one, there remains a single preeminent naval power, with America having assumed that role. And as mercantilism and its industrial rationale have receded as a national path to power, they have been replaced by a worldwide system of interdependence based on information—what one newsmagazine called the Age of Globality. Throughout these transitions reliance on the use of the seas as commercial bridges remains a constant. But arguably the most important parallel is the stubborn fact that naval forces still are an essential means of projecting national power where needed and when national security is threatened.

Those who think beyond short-term public wisdom realize that the importance of naval power remains a significant common denominator between Nelson's time and ours. As an important corollary, the ongoing question of how to shape the naval component of the nation's military strength requires something more than what one philosopher called ignorance in action.

At a Trafalgar Night affair in Washington, D.C., in October of 1970, then British Royal Navy Admiral of the Fleet, Sir Peter Hill-Norton, emphasized the value of looking to the past to understand the timeless verities associated with naval combat. He said, "It is a widely held fallacy that to look back on the past is not only unprofitable but a sign of decadence. Nothing could be further from the truth; none of us should make the mistake of thinking we have nothing to learn from history or its great men."[3]

Revisiting Nelson's career now provides us with a means to renew attention to the human aspect of naval power and, more specifically, to the character of those who will lead our naval forces in combat. It is a story that can't help but rivet one's attention; and it's provocative and dramatic and at times even seems implausible. But, more important, it's a story that provides a chance to learn basic lessons from brilliant combat successes. Combat leadership is primarily defined not by outward behavior but by success in battle.

The next eleven chapters provide an analytical look at Nelson's life, one that gets beyond what he did to the personal factors related to his combat successes and, in noteworthy instances, to his failures. It's not an academic study, but every effort has been made to bring accuracy and objectivity to the subject. It's hoped that the process of thinking about Nelson's complex, often contradictory, character will generate insights into the importance of successful combat leadership at sea. Chapters 2 and 3 provide a general overview of Nelson's life. Chapters 4, 5, 6, and 7 analyze specific aspects of his persona, and chapters 8 through 12 describe significant battles in which Nelson's combat leadership was shown in bold relief.

Cumulatively, the book makes it possible to draw lessons about the essential character of a unique warfighter, the person who was described by the early American sea power proponent, then Captain A. T. Mahan, in unusual terms. Mahan wrote in his 1897 biography of Nelson: "[H]e was the one man who in himself summed up and embodied the greatness of the possibilities which Sea Power comprehends, ... the man for whom genius and opportunity worked together."[4]

This contemporary view of Nelson's unique naval career isn't intended to bring new historical facts to light. It is an effort to provide new and needed insight into the factors, personal and external, that made him a uniquely successful combat leader, despite the reality that exceptional combat leadership is easier to detect than define. Ultimately this book is an attempt to encourage renewed commitment to maintaining a core group of combat leaders in the U.S. Navy who will win when American lives and values are at risk in battle.

One of the more striking of the many famous
Nelson portraits was painted by the court
painter of Austria, Heinrich Füger. The portrait
was done in Vienna during Nelson's return
from the Mediterranean in the company of
Lord and Lady Hamilton in 1800, and it shows
him in his full dress rear admiral's uniform.
Some of Nelson's contemporaries claimed that
the expression captures a hint of his intensity.
The portrait is part of the collection of the
Royal Naval Museum, Portsmouth, England.

Chapter 2

Chronology of Nelson's Life

Often chronologies are a side issue when studying the life of a famous person. In Horatio Nelson's case however, an awareness of the major events and the sequence of those events can be a special window on his character. For example, Nelson was not yet 21 years old when he was appointed a post-captain and deemed capable of commanding a Royal Navy warship. And the eight years between his appointment as a midshipman and his first command of a ship encompassed, to put it mildly, an interesting variety of personal learning experiences. In addition, it is thought provoking to contemplate that Nelson became a rear admiral before his fortieth birthday.

In a broad context Nelson's entire professional experience played out against a backdrop of historically important events, including the American and French Revolutions with their new ideas of political liberty. His career coincided with the rise of Napoleon to power and the weakening of monarchies as the leading form of national leadership. This broad context of Nelson's experience is as important as the individual events that, because of their drama and particular geopolitical impact, highlighted his career.

⸘☙⸙

1758, 29 September: Born at Burnham Thorpe Parsonage in Norfolk

1767, 26 December: Catherine, Nelson's mother, died

1770, November: Appointed, at age 12, as midshipman aboard HMS *Raisonnable*

1771 Shipped aboard a merchantman to the West Indies

1772 Returned to England

1773, June: Sailed with an expedition seeking an Arctic route to the Pacific

1773 Appointed midshipman aboard HMS *Seahorse*, sailed for the East Indies

1775 Fell ill from malaria

1775, April: The American Revolutionary War began

1776, 1 August: Returned to Britain

1777, April: Promoted to lieutenant and assigned to HMS *Lowestoffe*, served in West Indies

1778 France joined American War of Independence against Britain

1778, December: Appointed to his first command, HMS *Badger*

1779, June: Promoted to rank of post-captain at 20 years of age, and appointed to command HMS *Hinchinbroke*

1779 Spain joined France in war against Britain

1780, January: Led the naval portion of an unsuccessful attack on Fort San Juan in Nicaragua

1780, April: Appointed to command of HMS *Janus*, fell ill

1780, December: Returned to Britain

1781, August: Appointed to command of HMS *Albemarle,* took up escort duty in the Baltic

1781, October: General Washington achieved victory at Yorktown in the American Revolutionary War

1782, November: Joined Lord Hood's squadron off Quebec and New York City, then returned to the West Indies

1783, March: Failed in attempt to capture Turks Island in West Indies

1783, June: Returned to Britain

1783, September: The Treaty of Paris ending the American Revolution is signed

1783, October: Began four-month visit to St. Omer, France

1784, March: Appointed to command HMS *Boreas,* departed for West Indies

1785, May: Introduced to Frances Nisbet, his future wife, in Nevis, West Indies

1786, November: Began five-month assignment as Prince William Henry's aide

1787, March: Married to Frances Nisbet in Nevis

1787, July: Returned to Britain with his wife

1787 Placed on half-pay without an active Royal Navy assignment, lived at Burnham Thorpe

1789 French Revolution begins with the attack on the Bastille

1793, January: King Louis XVI of France is executed

1793, January: Appointed to command HMS *Agamemnon*

1793, February: War between Britain and Revolutionary France begins

1793, February: Departed for the Mediterranean

1793, September: Met with Sir William Hamilton, Ambassador to the Kingdom of the Two Sicilies, and his wife, Emma Lady Hamilton

1794, January: The Corsican naval campaign began

1794, July: Right eye injured at Calvi, resulted in loss of sight in the eye

1796 Alliance between Spain and France formed

1796, March: Appointed commodore, subsequently joined HMS *Captain*

1797, 14 February: The Battle of Cape St. Vincent took place, showed bold initiative, contributed to major British victory, subsequently promoted to rear admiral and created Knight of the Bath

1797, July: Involved in boat actions off Cadiz, including hand-to-hand combat

1797, 24 July: Assault on Santa Cruz, Tenerife failed, lost right arm as the result of a serious wound

1798, March: Hoisted rear admiral's flag on HMS *Vanguard*, joined fleet commanded by Admiral Sir John Jervis off Cadiz

1798, 1 August: Destroyed the French battle fleet in Aboukir Bay following a nerve-wracking search of the eastern Mediterranean, suffered a serious head wound

1798, 22 September: Returned to Naples to a hero's welcome, then nursed by Lady Hamilton

1798, November: Created Baron Nelson of the Nile

1798, December: Rescued Royal Family of the Kingdom of the Two Sicilies and Lord and Lady Hamilton from French Army advancing on Naples, transported them from Naples to Palermo

1799, June: Returned to Naples and cancelled truce between the British and the French and local rebels, summarily executes Admiral Caracciolo for assisting the French

1799, July: Disobeyed orders from Admiral Keith to sail for Minorca, criticized for being overly influenced by relationship with Lady Hamilton

1799, August: Created Duke of Brontë by King of the Kingdom of the Two Sicilies, given an estate in Sicily

1799, October: Napoleon arrived in France from Egypt

1799, December: Napoleon appointed First Consul of France

1800, November: Returned to England, traveled overland through European cities in the company of Lord and Lady Hamilton

1801, January: Promoted to vice admiral

1801, January: Separated from his wife

1801, February: Horatia, daughter of Nelson and Lady Hamilton, born

1801, 2 April: Defeated Danish forces in the Battle of Copenhagen

1801, May: Created Viscount Nelson of the Nile and Burnham Thorpe

1801, July: Took command of home defense force designed to protect Britain from invasion by Napoleon

1801, August: Led failed attack on French invasion forces assembled at Boulogne

1801, September: Purchased Merton Place as home for himself and Lord and Lady Hamilton

1801, October: Armistice between Britain and France signed

1801, October: Went on leave and joined Lord and Lady Hamilton at Merton

1802, March: Treaty of Amiens ending war between Britain and France, Spain and the Batavian Republic signed

1802, April: Nelson's father, Reverend Edmund Nelson, dies

1803, May: War with France renewed

1803, May: Appointed commander-in-chief in the Mediterranean, hoisted his flag in HMS *Victory*

1804 Commanded blockade of French fleet in Toulon

1804, December: Spain declared war against Britain

1805, April–July: Pursued French fleet to the West Indies and back

1805, August–September: Returned to Britain on leave, lived at Merton with Lady Hamilton

1805, September: Rejoined British fleet off Cadiz

1805, 21 October: Defeated the combined French-Spanish fleet at the Battle of Trafalgar, fatally wounded by a French sharp-shooter

1805, December: the *Victory* arrives in Portsmouth with Nelson's body

1806, 9 January: Buried directly under the great dome in St. Paul's Cathedral after an historic funeral

Chapter 3

A Comprehensive View

Horatio Nelson—even his name has a special aura. But what's behind the mythology that has been spun around the man? Was he the military genius he has been made out to be or just lucky in battle? Was his love affair with Lady Hamilton one of the great career motivators in his life or simply a risky emotional extravagance? Whatever else he was, he was a man who described himself with unerring accuracy as one who "cannot bear the thought of being absent from the scene of action."[5]

Nelson's Early Childhood

There was nothing epic about Nelson's birthplace, but it left an indelible stamp on his career. He was born in 1758 at Burnham Thorpe in Norfolk, close to the coast of England. Tom Pocock—considered to be one of the best of Nelson's modern biographers—described his boyhood surroundings: "When northerly gales blow from the sea, the beech trees above Burnham Thorpe heel and roll like masts. When the wind drops, the murmur of the surf can be heard from the Norfolk shore."[6]

In these surroundings, exploring the harbor and inlets that were so close to his home, the young Nelson began to develop the seaman's skills that were to be important to him during his career at sea. In those small waters at the sea's edge, he began to develop the instincts that elevated his seamanship to an important factor in battle.

Nelson was the sixth of eleven children. His father was the parson of Burnham Thorpe, and the two maintained a strong relationship until the Reverend Nelson died just three years before his son was killed at Trafalgar. That early and consistent religious influence was the foundation of Nelson's life-long and frequently expressed belief that God would determine the outcome of his battles and his life. Further it's clear from Nelson's writings that he was convinced that God was on his side. And there can be little doubt that his father, who was steeped in the classics, was a major factor in Nelson's ability to write with impact.

Those beliefs and that ability were never more evident than when he sat in the great cabin of his flagship, *Victory*, and wrote in anticipation of the Battle of Trafalgar: "May the Great God, whom I worship, grant to my Country, and for the benefit of Europe in general, a great and glorious Victory; and may no misconduct in any one tarnish it; and may humanity after Victory be the predominant feature in the British fleet. For myself individually, I commit my life to Him that made me, and may his blessings alight on my endeavours for serving my country faithfully. To Him I resign myself and the just cause which is entrusted to me to defend."[7]

The influence of Nelson's mother on his life, although considerably more short-lived than that of his father, was nonetheless very important. She died when he was only nine years old. When in his later years he described his relationship with her, it was in emotional terms. Her death when he was a young boy left an emotional void that surely contributed to his sensitive nature and to his response to the ego-enhancing attention of his paramour, Lady Hamilton. It's clear that his mother's hatred of the French also had a strong impact on him, an important influence during his entire adult life.

Apprenticeship

At twelve Nelson went to sea to begin a career in a harsh profession. And although he was not physically imposing, he compensated with a mental toughness that mitigated his physical shortcomings. That mental toughness was never more evident than when he repeatedly overcame serious battle wounds, including those suffered at Calvi on the island of Corsica where he lost the sight in his right eye, his wounds at the Battle of the Nile where he suffered a head laceration and severe concussion, and the loss of his right arm during the Battle of Santa Cruz.

Family influence had a lot to do with his opportunity for a naval career, as it did for most young men of his time who became officers in the Royal Navy. Nelson's uncle, Maurice Suckling, a well-connected senior captain in the Royal Navy, was the early role model and heroic family figure who drew Nelson towards a Royal Navy career. And it was Suckling's professional influence that set the early career course for the man who became Britain's greatest naval hero. It was his uncle's influence—referred to in Nelson's time as "interest"—at the Admiralty that provided at least the initial political leverage for Nelson's historic Royal Navy career.

Suckling's response when asked to accept young Horatio as a midshipman aboard his ship provides insights into both Nelson's early years and the dangers of his chosen profession. He wrote: "What has poor Horatio done, who is so weak, that he, above all the rest, should be sent to rough it out at sea?" Then Suckling added seemingly as an afterthought, "But let him come, and the first time we go into action a cannon ball may knock off his head, and provide for him at once."[8] Towards the end of his career, Nelson reprised his uncle's grim imagery in a letter to Lady Hamilton in 1803. He wrote: "I shall endeavour to do what is right, in every situation; and some ball may soon close all my accounts with this world of care and vexation!"[9]

Notwithstanding his uncle's pessimistic outlook, Nelson went on to become an exceptionally proficient seaman, an accomplishment that was considerably advanced by a brief but influential stretch in the British merchant marine. In later years, Nelson was to refer to his merchant marine experience as important in his understanding of and appreciation for the ordinary seamen who were the basic fiber of every ship.

Achieving Fame

One of the most obvious defining events in Nelson's naval career occurred at the Battle of Cape St. Vincent in February of 1797, where he demonstrated both bold initiative and raw physical courage. It was in the aftermath of the British victory at Cape St. Vincent, Nelson began to attract widespread attention—much of it generated by his own well-aimed and dramatic accounts of the battle—as someone with an exceptional ability to win in battle.

Because he was so successful, Nelson's actions, particularly his tactics, have been analyzed intensively by naval experts. For example, much has been made of his aggressiveness, which was a key element in his three most famous victories: the Battle of the Nile against the French in 1798, the Battle of Copenhagen against the Danes in 1801, and the Battle of Trafalgar against a combined French-Spanish fleet in 1805.

Receiving somewhat less attention than his effective combat tactics is the affection he had for those who served under him. At a time when sailors were routinely lashed to a hatch grating and beaten with the cat-o'-nine tails for relatively minor infractions, Nelson's regard for his sailors was unusual. And, although he was by no means considered a lax disciplinarian, those who sailed and fought alongside him recognized that he had a genuine regard for them. The result was a unique bond, one that created strong loyalty and fierce combat performance on the part of those who fought under his command. That union of loyalty and ferocity was a major contributor to Nelson's victories.

Robert Southey, the late eighteenth- and early nineteenth-century English writer who is considered to be the first true biographer of Nelson, focused on how strongly the ordinary seamen he commanded responded to his unusual brand of leadership. "Never was any commander more beloved," he wrote. According to Southey, as a result of this unusual personal connection, "He governed men by their reason and their affections: they knew that he was incapable of caprice or tyranny; and they obeyed him with alacrity and joy, because he possessed their confidence as well as their love."[10]

The emotional content of Nelson's personality also was a factor in his controversial love for Lady Hamilton. Despite an apparently stable marriage to Fanny Nisbet whom he met and married in Nevis, West Indies, when she was a young widow with a son, Nelson defied both social convention and moral restraints to pursue the notorious relationship with Emma Hamilton. The romance was triggered when Nelson returned to Naples after the Battle of the Nile. There Lady Hamilton—who held forth as the influential wife of Sir William Hamilton, Britain's ambassador to the court of the Kingdom of the Two Sicilies—helped nurse Nelson back to health. She also led the nearly hysterical adulation in Naples of "The Hero of the Nile."

Nelson pursued the emotional relationship with the same intensity he took into battle, and at times, it cost him in terms of his reputation and his career. But when the crises came, the Admiralty and Whitehall repeatedly put aside other considerations and called upon him as the best naval combat leader they had.

Although Nelson's biographers all recognize his tremendous popularity with the British general public of his time, not all recognize the close connection of that popularity to his career successes. Apparently Nelson himself did. His letters and journals did not dwell on the subject, but they do reflect that he understood the fact that favorable public opinion was the constant that kept him going when his support wavered elsewhere. For example in a letter to Earl of St. Vincent he wrote, "[W]e know, from experience, that more depends upon opinion than the facts themselves."[11]

Seeing Beyond Success

Observations like those also strongly suggest that Nelson didn't fight simply to win. He understood the long-range strategic implications, which were momentous, of his military victories. While Napoleon was having his way militarily on the Continent, it was Nelson's brilliance, plus the relentless sea-keeping and ferocious combat performance of the Royal Navy, that kept Napoleon from invading Britain and gaining complete control of the western world of the time.

The long-term historical influence of Nelson's naval achievements undoubtedly shaped the course of history, and a sense of that historical impact was one of the driving forces in his career. Honor and acclaim certainly were major drives for him as his career gained momentum, but it was peace in Europe and the defeat of a perceived tyrant that increasingly occupied his thoughts in the latter stages of his life.

An important historical aftermath of Nelson's stunning victories was that an understanding of the importance of sea power was accelerated for future generations. One of the results of this enhanced appreciation for the role of sea power was seen in America's expanded use of naval power towards the close of the nineteenth century. In the Spanish-American war for example, American naval power was used not simply as a means for defending national coastal areas and commerce but as the means of achieving global extension of national power.

Today the famous sixteen-story monument of Nelson in central London's Trafalgar Square, his meticulously restored flagship, HMS *Victory*, in Portsmouth, England, and hundreds of other sites around the world memorialize Nelson. These sites are as much reminders of the ongoing relevance of sea power as they are memorials to a unique naval commander.

Chapter 4

Character Counts in Combat

T he idea of character—a unique combination of qualities that distinguishes a person—has been around for along time. It is found in ancient Greek and Latin literature. In Middle English it was defined as an imprint on the soul. The philosopher Goethe pointed out that character develops "in the full current of life"—for Nelson that current was swift and violent. Another philosopher, Jacques Maritain, put character in a different perspective: "We don't love qualities, we love persons; sometimes by reason of their defects as well as their qualities." And Nelson certainly had both defects and strong qualities. F. Scott Fitzgerald cut to the core when he wrote, "Action is character"; Nelson would have liked that blunt bit of wisdom.

In examining how Nelson's character developed and how it related to his effectiveness as a combat leader, there are some difficulties. Perhaps the greatest of these is the sheer complexity of his person. For example he demonstrated—at times almost simultaneously—both extreme harshness and patient forgiveness. His approval in 1799 of the hanging of Admiral Caracciolo and the throwing of his body into the harbor of Naples was a shocking example of the former. In the same year, the manner in which he commuted the death sentence of a young Royal Marine private who was convicted of striking an officer was an example of the latter.

On the plus side for examining Nelson's character is the fact that the events of his life were momentous enough to clearly reveal important aspects of his personality. Whether it was hand-to-hand combat between two boat crews or the sweeping chaos of major fleet battles, the events of Nelson's life were dramatically defining. In addition, his life is so well recorded, in both his own dispatches and letters and the innumerable biographies and analyses written about him, there is a wealth of evidence to study.

Character Linked to Doctrine

The quintessential warfighter General George Patton alluded to the important link between combat doctrine and character when he wrote, "In war, the only sure defense is offense; and the efficiency of offense depends on the warlike souls of those conducting it."[12] This observation not only reveals a core element of Patton's personal combat doctrine, aggressiveness, but also points out a requirement for "warlike souls," the special personalities needed to apply his doctrine successfully. Patton's observation emphasizes that, no matter how innovative or progressive it may be, the soundest of doctrines is not enough. It must be fused to a personality that can drive it to victory in the field.

It's possible to identify many, if not all, of the important personal qualities that combined to elevated Nelson's character to the level Patton's observation implies. They include physical and mental courage, aggressiveness, deeply held religious beliefs, patriotism, knowledge of the sea, and regard for those he commanded. These qualities may not have made Nelson a perfect person but, without a doubt, they combined to form the core of an inspiring leader and a combat winner.

Physical Courage

Although Nelson was of average stature and suffered constantly from seasickness and wounds—several of which came close to ending his career—his physical bravery exceeded his appearance, and it was evident from his early years. Among the early accounts of this courage was an incident during a voyage of exploration toward the North Pole aboard the sloop, HMS *Carcass* in 1773. Nelson, then a 15-year-old midshipman and already a veteran of several years at sea in a 64-gun ship-of-the-line, had begged his way into being signed on as coxswain of the captain's gig.

One night during a mid-watch he and a shipmate slipped away from the *Carcass*, which was trapped in an ice field, to pursue a polar bear. When Nelson's musket misfired he was prepared to attack the bear using his musket as a club. Fortunately a separation in the ice and a recall signal from his captain—reportedly not even slightly amused by the incident—saved Nelson for later, more geopolitically significant combat.

Many other conspicuous demonstrations of physical bravery followed. For example during a night action off Cadiz when his boat crew was greatly outnumbered by the enemy, he led a desperate and successful hand-to-hand struggle. This incident became an enduring part of the fame that has grown around Nelson's life during the past two centuries. In another instance he refused to conceal his identity from French sharpshooters by covering his conspicuous medals and awards at the beginning of the Battle of Trafalgar. That refusal may well have contributed to his death at that battle.

The roots of his exceptional physical courage were deep and had varied origins. Nelson himself touched on the subject in a letter to Lady Hamilton that revealed one particularly interesting source of his courage. His words are particularly provocative in light of the cultural changes among Western nations during the past 50 years. He wrote: "It is your sex that rewards us; it is your sex who cherish our memories; and you, my dear, honoured friend, are, believe me, the *first* and best of your sex!" [13]

An apocryphal story told by one of his grandmothers strongly suggests that not all of Nelson's courage was based on societal factors. Her tale described how Nelson and an older companion lost their way in the woods. The older boy left Nelson, stranded on the wrong side of a small river, to fend for himself. When the older boy found his way back home and Horatio did not appear for dinner, a search party went out to find him. They discovered him waiting calmly beside the river, exactly where his companion had left him. His grandmother scolded him and asked why fear had not driven him home. Nelson's reply was, "I never saw fear. What is it?"

Mental Toughness

Besides great physical courage, Nelson possessed a mental toughness that did not allow for fear of failure. He not only risked his life in combat, his actions, including those in combat, often involved big political risks. In the process, he repeatedly put both life and career on the line. This refusal to be influenced by the consequences of failure was vividly demonstrated, for example, by his taking independent action during an early, critical stage of the Battle of Cape St. Vincent. In that action Nelson turned his ship out of formation, a maneuver that precipitated the close combat desired by Nelson's commander-in-chief. Over the years historians have recorded Nelson's action at Cape St. Vincent as disobedience to an order. However one recent account makes a credible claim that it was a risky initiative rather than disobedience to orders.[14] In either event, Nelson's action required him to chose boldness over a safer course. Later at the Battle of Copenhagen, there was absolutely no doubt that Nelson ignored an order from his commander-in-chief on the way to victory. Although in hindsight his boldness and departures from orders generally were considered essential to the victories that followed, it required great courage at the time by significantly raising Nelson's personal stakes in the battles. His departures from orders and bold initiative changed the battle equation for him from win-lose to glory-disgrace. He often referred to that extreme equation in statements, such as, "All or none, is my motto."

This willingness to risk all, both physically and politically, can be explained in part by an event Nelson himself described. After a near-fatal illness he was returning to England from Bombay in the frigate HMS *Dolphin*, when he experienced something that set the tone of his career. He described it later in his life: "After a long and gloomy reverie, in which I almost wished myself overboard, a sudden glow of patriotism was kindled within me and presented my King and Country as my patron. 'Well then,' I exclaimed, 'I will be a hero and, confiding in Providence, I will brave every danger.'"[15]

Aggressiveness

One of the most important manifestations of Nelson's physical and mental courage was his aggressiveness in battle. This aspect of his character was central to his now famous and almost universally successful tactics, which were designed to seize and maintain the initiative in battle. It was tersely summed up in a statement made on more than one occasion by Nelson himself, "[T]he boldest measures are the safest."[16]

Nelson's aggressiveness is particularly interesting in light of Royal Navy doctrine of the time, which was predominantly conservative. And when evaluated in the context of his battles, Nelson's consistent option for attack is even more remarkable. At the Battle of Copenhagen for example, his pursuit of aggressive tactics led him to ignore a direct order to retire that was sent from his fleet commander, Sir Hyde Parker. When Parker made the signal Nelson's reaction was an emphatic, "Leave off action! Now, damn me if I do."[17]

It's also important to note that Nelson succeeded in linking his purposeful aggressiveness with perseverance, and in fact the combination of the two qualities was repeatedly proven to be greater than their sum. Arguably the best example of this critical combination was demonstrated when Nelson chased French Admiral Villeneuve through the Mediterranean and Atlantic and endured several years of arduous blockading to finally press home his climactic attack at Trafalgar. Nelson's hunting down the French fleet leading to the

Battle of the Nile was an earlier example of his powerful blend of dogged perseverance with an aggressive combat doctrine.

Religious Conviction

Nelson held deep religious beliefs, reflecting his early upbringing as the son of a parson. References to the will of God permeate his letters, memos, and dispatches. For example Nelson's last diary—begun as he left Lady Hamilton and his young daughter, Horatia, to serve his "King and Country" in his final battle—provides one of the most dramatic expressions of this aspect of his character. The diary begins with a reference to leaving "all which I hold dear in this world," and continues, "May the Great God whom I adore enable me to fulfill the expectations of my Country; and if it is His good pleasure that I should return, my thanks will never cease being offered up ... If it is His good providence to cut short my days upon earth, I bow with the greatest submission, relying that He will protect those so dear to me, that I may leave behind."[18] That diary entry also reveals how tightly Nelson linked his religious beliefs to his sense of duty. And it identifies a type of fatalism that never compromised his proactive nature, but instead allowed him to face the shocks of battle calmly.

Another important facet of Nelson's religious conviction is that it provided a powerful rationale for his violent profession. Napoleon and the post-monarchy governments of France not only rejected monarchy as a form of government, they added a strong antireligious tenor to their fervor for change. Thus for Nelson, he was fighting against a nation that, in his opinion, was building a radical and threatening new form of government. It was, he believed, a movement that attacked the basic foundation of society, the belief in God. For Nelson fighting against France was a classic case being on the side of God. In modern terms, he fought a just war.

Patriotism

Nelson's regard for those elected to govern his nation and those appointed to run his navy was not always high, but his love of country was. There was for example never a question of the "rightness" of his country's opposition to France and its allies, and this conviction had several bases. One basis was the conviction that France was unfairly trying to compromise Britain's legitimate influence in European matters. Matched with that politically based consideration was a powerful ideological factor. As already alluded to, Nelson believed that republicanism, particularly the excesses represented by France after its revolution, was basically an immoral and corrupt form of government. It was an evil that had to be overcome.

This side of Nelson's patriotism was particularly evident during his tours as a fleet commander in the Mediterranean. It was clear from his writings during those periods that he saw his responsibilities as more than the pragmatic securing and retaining of allies for Britain, the denial of allies to France, and the securing of naval bases for the Royal Navy. It also was a matter of protecting a parliamentary monarchy from the evils of revolutionary republicanism. This impulse to defend against republicanism also was extended to less liberal monarchies, such as the Kingdom of the Two Sicilies. There was a certain amount of irony in that latter instance since he had voiced the opinion, in writing, that the Kingdom of the Two Sicilies was "a country of fiddlers and poets, whores and scoundrels."

One of the personal translations of Nelson's patriotism—something more closely related to ideology than politics—was his unequivocal hatred of Napoleon. He revealed the strength of those feelings in a letter written aboard the *Victory* in 1804: "Buonaparte's tongue is that of a serpent oiled. Nothing shall be wanting on my part to frustrate the designs of this common disturber of the human race."[19] In an earlier letter he identified a primary root of this emotional attitude: "I would not, upon any consideration, have a Frenchman in the Fleet, except as a prisoner .... Forgive me; but my mother hated the French."[20]

There was an additional, commercial, basis for Nelson's patriotism that may seem odd by today's standards but that was relevant during his career. This special dimension of his patriotism was rooted in two practices: prize money awarded for captures of ships and money awards by British commercial groups for naval victories.

Royal Navy ship captains and admirals of Nelson's era pursued their careers at least partially in hope of capturing lucrative prizes; many accumulated substantial fortunes in the process. Nelson frequently protested with considerable justification that honor and duty, not prize money, were his primary motivations; and that claim can be supported by his actions during his career. But occasionally he brought the subject up in a context that revealed his appreciation for what the capture of valuable prizes could mean to his and his family's wellbeing. In fact, it was very clear in the case of at least two of his contemporaries, Admiral Sir John Orde and Admiral Lord Keith, that Nelson harbored great animosity towards them because they had been positioned to reap prize money that he, Nelson, should have garnered.

The money awards by British commercial groups, usually accompanied other tangible symbols of gratitude such as silver plate, were made on the basis of the Royal Navy's protection of private property and assets. The British East India Company, for example, was one of the groups that made significant awards to Royal Navy ship captains who distinguished themselves in the protection of valuable convoys. Lloyd's of London, who insured many of the cargoes carried in British merchant ships of the time, also was prominent in this practice. And today Lloyd's, which emerged from the wars with Napoleon as a world-renowned society of underwriters, maintains a unique minimuseum of Nelson memorabilia that can, with appropriate arrangements, be viewed at their London headquarters.[21]

Knowledge of the Sea

Nelson's sea-going professionalism began with his youthful experiences with small boats and harbor navigation that resulted, in his words, in his becoming "confident of myself among rocks and sands." As he advanced to offshore navigation and blue-water seamanship in the British merchant service he became, again in his own words, "a practical seaman." The result of his thorough seagoing schooling in seamanship was that he had confidence in combat situations that could have intimidated others.

This part of his character played a significant role for example in his victories at the Battles of the Nile, Copenhagen, and Trafalgar. At the Nile and Copenhagen, Nelson had to contend with shoal waters with which he and his captains were not intimately familiar, a circumstance that any seaman would find daunting. Add the chaos of battle to the equation and Nelson's skill and nerve are even more impressive. In the case of Trafalgar, Nelson *read* the state of the seas and the sky and realized that a major storm was imminent. His orders to his flag captain to anchor after the battle were repeated even as he was dying. As it turned out, the battle was immediately followed by a ferocious storm that took many additional lives.

A Special Regard for Those He Commanded

There were many brave and aggressive leaders in the Royal Navy of Nelson's time. But the special connection he had with his men and officers, although impossible to quantify, was a very important part of what raised him above his contemporaries and made him such a fearsome leader in battle. Whether it was concern for the common seamen, attention to the welfare of his midshipmen, or appreciation for the abilities of his captains, Nelson was open in his regard and respect for them all, and they reciprocated. As a result, and most importantly, they fought ferociously for him. This dimension of Nelson's relationship with all levels of his subordinates went far beyond merely getting obedience to orders, it added a huge increment to his effectiveness as a warfighter.

One of Nelson's most highly regarded biographers, Carola Oman, described a particularly emotional expression of the love those who served with Nelson had for him. She wrote: "The final incident of Lord Nelson's funeral ... was undisciplined and unrehearsed. It had been set down that the men of the *Victory* were to furl the shot-rent colours which they had borne in the procession and lay them upon the coffin; but when the moment came, they seized upon the ensign, largest of the *Victory*'s three flags, and tearing a great piece off it, quickly managed so that every man transferred to his bosom a memorial of his great and favourite commander."[22]

The Catalysts

Before leaving an examination of the elements of Nelson's character that contributed to his successes in battle, it's worth recognizing that those elements required outside enablers. Two are particularly interesting, Britain's political and naval leadership of his time, and British public opinion during his lifetime. In the former case there were times when the support from those areas was none too firm. Many at Whitehall and the Admiralty would have been happy to see Nelson retire years before Trafalgar. To them Nelson was a threat and an annoyance, and they bitterly resented many of the assignments he received from senior officers like Admiral Sir John Jervis. The Battles of Cape St. Vincent and Copenhagen might have been victories for Britain, but they were achieved by extraordinary tactics that, in at least one instance, included a departure from orders. For many at the Admiralty that struck at the very foundations of the Royal Navy and their considerable egos. Fortunately, there were others at the Admiralty, notably Admiral Jervis, who recognized Nelson's unique capabilities as a combat leader.

In the case of Whitehall, it was fortunate for Britain and all Europe that the political scales there never fully tipped against Nelson. He was at times officially snubbed, and in some instances, he was denied full official recognition for his achievements. The aftermath of the Battle of Copenhagen was a noteworthy example of such pointed neglect. But he was, nevertheless, called upon by his country at critical junctures in its history. And very likely, despite the generally high quality of the Royal Navy's senior leadership at the time, there was no other naval combat leader who could have achieved what Nelson did.

Chapter 5

The Power of Love

Nelson was prone to falling in love. When he was 23 years old, Mary Simpson in Quebec, Canada was the object of his affections. Two years later, a Miss Andrews, who was visiting St. Omer, France, at the same time as Nelson, was the object of his ardor. In both instances, Nelson convinced himself that he had met the woman he wanted to marry but circumstances intervened.

There also was an affair in 1794–95, seven years after his marriage, with Adelaide Correglia, an Italian opera singer in Leghorn, who coincidentally spied for Nelson against the French. One of Nelson's fellow officers referred to Correglia as a "Dolly"—at that time, a euphemism for a mistress—and observed disapprovingly that Nelson was making a fool of himself with her. But it was his wife, Fanny, and his paramour, Lady Hamilton, who were the strongest female influences on him as a warfighter, each at a different time, each with a starkly different personality, and each in a different way.

The Young Widow

When Nelson was introduced to Frances Nisbet in May of 1785, he had been a post-captain for almost six years. His naval and merchant marine service included the West Indies, the Atlantic, the Arctic, the East Indies, and the Baltic. He was mature in the ways of the sea but at age 26 perhaps less so in matters of love. His future wife, only a few months older than he, had been married to a doctor on Nevis in the West Indies. Because of her husband's poor health they had returned to England where he died. Fanny then returned to Nevis where she had spent most of her life. Back in the West Indies she took over as hostess for her uncle, John Herbert, president of Nevis. In that role, she supervised the entertaining of his guests and the management of the household staff.

A female friend of Fanny's, who had encountered Nelson at a dinner before he and Fanny met, described him in ambiguous terms; she was neither the first nor the last to do so. On the one hand, he seemed to her to be unusually reserved and stern—even strange. But at times she also found him to be lively, particularly during the toasts to the Royal Family. He also showed signs, according to Fanny's friend, of having a superior mind. All of which, she said, made it impossible to fathom his true character. She suggested to Fanny that if she had been present she "would have made something of him."[23] Nelson for his part was uncharacteristically subdued in his initial description of Fanny, referring to her simply as a young widow.

Despite the unspectacular beginning of the relationship, a genuine affection between Fanny and her husband-to-be developed. She provided the female companionship for which Nelson had repeatedly demonstrated a need. It is also clear that he saw her as a source of praise, the psychological nourishment that his ego craved. For example, after the Corsican Campaign, at a time in 1794 when he was feeling officially neglected, he wrote to her: "I rejoice that my conduct gives you pleasure."[24]

Fanny and Nevis also represented a refuge for Nelson in the Leeward Islands at a time when he—through strict enforcement of

Britain's Navigation Acts—had made himself extremely unwelcome in most of the West Indies' ports. Even Fanny's seven-year-old son, Josiah, was a factor in the developing romance. Fanny's uncle provided interesting insight into that aspect of the relationship when he wrote of discovering Nelson playing under a table with Josiah. The amusing scene described by Herbert also provided insight into some of the sharp contrasts in Nelson's character. At one point, he wrote: "Great God! If I did not find that great little man, of whom everybody is so afraid, playing . . . under the dining table with Mrs Nisbet's child." [25]

For Fanny's part, the relationship represented a return to the security of marriage and the prospect of an attentive stepfather for her son. And Nelson's elaborate protestations of love and respect added a note of romance. However in the perspective of time, Nelson's early, effusive correspondence with Fanny showed his tendency towards exaggerated feelings. In addition, his letter writing seemed suspiciously like the strivings of a man creating an ideal woman in his own mind, a person who did not exist in reality. At one point he wrote to his brother, William: "Her sense, polite manners, and to you I may say, beauty, you will much admire." [26] Later he wrote to Fanny in the same mode: "You have given me a proof that your goodness increases by time." And in the same letter, with what would become painful irony, he wrote: "These I trust will ever be my sentiments; if they are not . . . it will be my folly that occasions it." [27] The last part of that statement takes on a sad note in light of Nelson's eventual, and seemingly insensitive, separation from his wife.

Nelson proposed in August 1785, and Fanny accepted. For the next 18 months they maintained a warm and active correspondence, and on March 11, 1787, they were married on Nevis, with Prince William giving the bride away. In July they returned to England, Nelson in his own ship, HMS *Boreas*, and Fanny in a West Indiaman. Fanny went to Burnham Thorpe and Nelson remained aboard the *Boreas* until the ship was taken out of active service, leaving Nelson without a Royal Navy assignment. Finally in November of 1787, Nelson and Fanny took up married life together at Burnham Thorpe.

An Unfavorable Climate

Both Fanny and Nelson suffered from the environment at Burnham Thorpe, one literally and the other figuratively. Fanny suffered from the raw winter weather of Norfolk, a bleak and penetratingly cold environment that contrasted with the lush warmth and vivid colors of the Caribbean. In addition, she suffered from the limited social contact at Burnham Thorpe, which contrasted so sharply with the vibrant social life she led as hostess for her uncle in Nevis. Nelson for his part suffered from the acute frustration of naval unemployment.

For five years they remained in those circumstances, until the on-again-off-again war between France and Britain resumed in 1793. At that point Nelson was finally given command of a ship, HMS *Agamemnon*. Fanny's unhappiness at the departure of her husband was doubtlessly not mitigated by the fact that 13-year-old Josiah sailed with his stepfather as a midshipman. By the time Nelson was back at sea, formality and resignation had replaced the early warmth and enthusiasm of the relationship. And his correspondence about missing items in the baggage Fanny had packed for him revealed undisguised irritation with her failures with the important, to Nelson, details of being an efficient and supportive "navy wife."

During the next four-plus years, Nelson saw a lot of active and dangerous service. He participated in the Corsican naval campaign, and at Calvi a wound cost him the sight of his right eye, a circumstance he downplayed with Fanny. His actions at the Battle of Cape St. Vincent drew considerable public acclaim for boldness and bravery. The Battle of Santa Cruz in July of 1797 quickly followed those two events and, in contrast to his previous combat successes, was a crushing defeat for Nelson. During that battle he suffered a wound that resulted in the loss of his right arm. His life was saved only by Josiah's quick action in getting his stepfather back to the *Agamemnon* and the surgeon's attention.

Those years between Nelson's return to active service and his return home after the Battle of Santa Cruz were critical to the marriage. Nelson was pursuing his chosen career with distinction and courage and no doubt expected enthusiastic praise, and presumably children, from his wife. But Fanny, despite expressions of admiration for his exploits, too often seemed to emphasize the risks he was taking and his absence from home. And there had been no children. Her concerns for Nelson's safety were frequently expressed more as complaints than as part of the approbation he craved. A phrase from a letter she wrote after the Battle of Cape St. Vincent represents this tone. She began the long and newsy letter by referring to her reactions to his exploits: "My anxiety was far beyond my powers of expression .... Altogether my dearest husband, my sufferings were great."[28]

From Nelson's perspective Fanny was simply not living up to the image of her he had created initially. When Nelson returned home after the Battle of Santa Cruz, Fanny responded with tenderness and attentiveness to his slow-healing amputation. Notwithstanding Nelson's physical suffering during this period, it probably was the most fulfilling time for both in their doomed marriage. But by the time he returned to the Mediterranean in March of 1798 aboard HMS *Vanguard,* the relationship had gone through two periods of steady deterioration, one at Burnham Thorpe and one while Nelson was at sea. The stage was set for a more passionate relationship, and the female lead for the role arrived in the person of Lady Hamilton.

A Woman of Amiable Manners

Nelson first met Lady Hamilton in Naples in 1793 where she held forth as the wife of Sir William Hamilton, British ambassador to the Kingdom of the Two Sicilies. Lady Hamilton, the daughter of a Cheshire blacksmith, had arrived at her station in life with an interesting past which included domestic service in London and probably prostitution as well. She had been, among other things, an actress, and the mistress of Sir William's nephew, Charles Greville.

Greville had advanced Emma's education in the arts among his circle of acquaintances, including the well-known artists, Romney and Reynolds, both of whom painted her portrait.

While Emma was still his mistress, Greville brought her to Naples for a visit to his uncle. Subsequently he provided her as a "gift" to him. Sir William was many years her senior and eventually was sufficiently taken with Emma's intelligence and charm to marry her. As Lady Hamilton she quickly became a favorite at court in Naples and the particular confidant of the Queen. In that unofficial but importantly influential position of power she was a particularly effective instrument of British interests at the court.

In a letter to Fanny, Nelson's reference to that first meeting may have seemed innocuous, but it portended troubled waters for their marriage. He wrote: "Lady Hamilton has been wonderfully kind and good to Josiah. She is a young women of amiable manners, and who does honour to the station to which she is raised."[29] It's easy to imagine how, with her husband several thousand miles distant, such a reference triggered doubts and fears for Fanny; the fact that Lady Hamilton was being "wonderfully kind and good" to Josiah surely didn't help matters.

Five years later in August of 1798 Nelson achieved one of his most brilliant victories at the Battle of the Nile. After hunting a French invasion fleet for months, he finally located the battle force in Aboukir Bay, where he won a bloody, overwhelming victory for Britain. But he did so at an enormous personal price. He was physically and emotionally exhausted by the constant stress of hunting the French, and during the ferocious battle he received a head wound that left him with the lingering symptoms of a very serious concussion. He returned to Naples in that condition in mid-September.

The welcome Nelson received there would have been overwhelming under any circumstances; hysterical is not too strong an adjective to describe his reception. He was celebrated in court and in public as the savior of the Kingdom of the Two Sicilies, indeed of all Europe. And Lady Hamilton was at the center of the celebrations, publicly praising him as a demigod. Privately she also cared for Nelson, helping to return him to a measure of health. It was the beginning of a relationship that evolved into one of the most infamous love affairs in history—one that has been both ridiculed and celebrated in literature.

The affair defied many conventions, including the fact that Sir William Hamilton was completely comfortable with his wife's relationship with Nelson and considered Nelson to be a good friend. Nelson's frequently referred to his relationship with Lady Hamilton in terms of friendship. Over time it became known in many circles in less lofty terms.

The Brave and the Fair

Nelson was moral, possessed strong religious beliefs, and had deeply romantic attitudes about women. These factors in combination led him to reject simply maintaining Lady Hamilton as a mistress, which would have been consistent with a common practice of the time. In fact he purchased a home at Merton where he and the Hamiltons could live together. His love for Lady Hamilton was not peripheral to his life, it was central. And as far as we know he was faithful to her during their relationship. As a result he thought of her as his wife. He naively expected others to see her in the same way and demonstrated considerable animosity towards those who did not. Consistent with that mind set, he separated from Lady Nelson in January of 1801.

In September of 1805, just before his final victory and death at Trafalgar, he wrote to Lady Hamilton reflecting his attitude about the relationship: "I entreat, my dear Emma, that you will cheer up; and we will look forward to many, many happy years, and be surrounded by our children's children. God almighty can, when he pleases, remove the impediment."[30] Adding to the tragic element of the situation, the impediment, Lady Nelson, was in fact a loyal and loving wife, despite her failure to match her husband's initial image of her. Until his death, Fanny pursued a reconciliation with her husband.

One of the clearest and most dramatic expressions of Lady Hamilton's importance to Nelson's combat persona was articulated in a letter written to her shortly before the Battle of Copenhagen in 1801. In the letter Nelson reveals the strength of his romanticism: "I know you are so true and loyal and Englishwoman, that you would hate those who would not stand forth in defence of our King, Laws, and Religion, and all that is dear to us. It is your sex that make us go forth; and seem to tell us—'None but the brave deserve the fair!' and, if we fall, we still live in the hearts of those females who are dear to us ... I have been the world around, and in every corner of it, and never saw your equal, or even one which could be put in comparison with you. You know how to reward virtue, honour, and courage . . . ."[31] Those words speak volumes about how Nelson's love for Lady Hamilton had become a significant motivation in battle, a powerful combination of a romantic view of combat and classic chivalry.

Another significant factor in Nelson's regard for Lady Hamilton was his belief that, while her husband was ambassador to the Kingdom of the Two Sicilies, she performed unusually important services for the British government. Those services in British interests included providing unique influence with an important ally and facilitating the resupply of Nelson's ships before the Battle of the Nile. Lady Hamilton's political acumen and obvious intelligence both contributed to her attractiveness for Nelson. He went so far as to propose to Whitehall on several occasions, including in his final will, that she be provided a pension for her services to Britain and its ally in Naples. Although Nelson described how Lady Hamilton had been "of the very greatest service to our King and Country" with considerable specificity in a codicil to his will, the British government never acceded to his request.

Nelson's love affair with Lady Hamilton was at times ridiculed in the press. It also was strongly criticized among his many friends and supporters who believed it to be damaging to his career and cruelly unfair to Lady Nelson. However, Nelson remained stubbornly undeterred. Once committed to the relationship, he pursued it with the same steadfast determination he brought to his professional career. And although the affair surely was hurtful to his wife and at times undercut his professional and political support, it clearly provided emotional strength that helped Nelson through his most stressful periods.

This profound impact of Nelson's love for Lady Hamilton on his personality was dramatically displayed in a poem he wrote to her aboard HMS *San Josef* in February 1801. The poem was part of a letter written just before the Battle of Copenhagen and just after the emotional events of January, which included his separation from Lady Nelson and the birth of his and Lady Hamilton's daughter, Horatia.

> *A heart susceptible, sincere, and true;*
> *A heart, by fate, and nature, torn in two:*
> *One half, to duty and his country due;*
> *The other, better half, to love and you!* [32]

In addition to revealing the depth of his feelings for his paramour, Nelson's verse demonstrated yet another of the conflicts of his personality. In this case it was his need for love contrasted with his powerful sense of duty that was manifested. But in final analysis, it appears that Nelson actually was able to convert what could have been an internal conflict compromising his warfighter's mentality into something that actually strengthened him for battle.

As it turned out one of the most famous romances of modern history was a tragedy of epic proportions. Nelson did not live to return to his beloved Merton to enjoy the idyllic life he envisioned with Lady Hamilton. And Lady Hamilton died in poverty in France in 1815, a victim of her extravagant living and her inability to cope with Nelson's death at Trafalgar. It was an ending for early Greek dramatists but not one for nineteenth- or twentieth century writers—perhaps the reason there is relatively little attention devoted to the sad conclusion of the romance between Nelson and Lady Hamilton.

A letter to Lady Hamilton, found open on Nelson's desk aboard the *Victory* after the battle of Trafalgar, was delivered to her at Merton after the event. On it she penned several grief-stricken lines—as it turned out for posterity—that foretold her own future misery and Nelson's future fame: "Oh miserable, wretched Emma. Oh glorious and happy Nelson."

Chapter 6

Duty of a Sea Officer

N elson's sense of duty was a powerful force in his career. It also was a significant factor in his amazing combat achievements. This ongoing influence of Nelson's commitment to carrying out his duty was apparent from the earliest stages of his career to the last moments of his life, and he frequently referred to the subject in his dispatches and letters. He described duty as the "great business of the Sea-officer," and he did not hesitate to lecture those with whom he corresponded on the subject.

But there was a pervasive rational element in his exceptional devotion to duty, something that, at times, translated into selective obedience to orders. For example, when the primary objectives of his assignment were in conflict with immediate orders, Nelson believed that his duty lay in achieving the former. Thus, despite his opinion that "to obey orders is all perfection," he often perceived his duty to lie in career-risking departures from his orders. That inclination regularly drew him into a difficult situation, something he described as "a confounded scrape." One of the earliest and most revealing of these "scrapes" grew out of a West Indies assignment as a young post-captain.

Caribbean Confrontation

In March of 1784, Nelson was appointed commanding officer of HMS *Boreas*. During the following several years, he precipitated and then perpetuated a confrontation with the British administrators and merchants of the West Indies. The problem involved the notorious lack of enforcement of Britain's Navigation Acts in those islands. The Navigation Acts were a series of laws motivated by Britain's mercantilist economic policy. One element of that policy required a nation to export more than it imported. As a result, Parliament passed the Navigation Acts to protect British commerce and industry from foreign competition. Thus, America's newly won independence ended her right to trade directly in the British West Indies.

For the British merchants and administrators in the West Indies however, it was not the government policy conceived in London but their own economic self-interest that shaped their commercial relationships with the trade-minded merchants of America. The result was a brisk trade conducted while the local authorities in the British West Indian colonies looked the other way. American ships would frequently enter a port on the pretext of requiring repairs to damage that threatened their safety at sea. They would then conduct their business while "making repairs." Nelson refused to ignore the illegal traffic and actively frustrated its conduct, enraging merchants, civic officials, and even the shore-based Royal Navy officers who were part of the permanent local establishments.

He wrote frequently and passionately about what he saw as an outrageous situation. On one occasion he pronounced: "Whilst I have the honour to command an English Man-of-War, I never shall allow myself to be subservient to the will of any Governor, nor cooperate with him in doing *illegal acts*."[33] In another letter, he was more specific about protecting British commercial interests: "I was appointed by the Commander-in-Chief to the Station at these islands to protect the Commerce of Great Britain, which I have endeavoured to do by every means in my power."[34]

One of the exchanges that grew out of the situation was with the Captain-General of the Islands, who patronizingly rebuked Nelson's perceived impertinence by writing that "old generals were not in the habit of taking advice from young gentlemen." Nelson's reply was a verbal version of his combat aggressiveness: "I have the honour, Sir, of being as old as the Prime Minister of England, and I think myself as capable of commanding one of His Majesty's Ships as that Minister is of governing the State." That type of verbal broadside was not well received by those who were feeling the direct economic penalties of Nelson's actions.

As a result of the situation, Nelson believed that he was confronted with a choice between obeying his local orders, or obeying the laws of Parliament. And he frequently couched the situation in those black-and-white terms. Foretelling how he would react to later, somewhat similar dilemmas, he chose adherence to the larger duty over conformity to his more immediate orders. This willingness to determine on his own where his greatest duty lay, combined with his aggressive attitude, made him very unpopular among the West Indies shore establishment and even with some merchants and officials back in Britain.

Because of the tensions that he created, there were very few places where he could safely go ashore in the West Indies. That made for a very contentious and tedious tour of duty. Of longer-range importance were the legal ramifications of Nelson's interpretation of his duty as the commanding officer of a Royal Navy ship in the West Indies. But when the West Indian merchants attempted to sue him for their business losses, Nelson's interpretation of his duty—as unpopular and controversial as it had been—was upheld in Britain. This vindication no doubt provided early reinforcement to his willingness to depart from an order in order to comply with what he perceived as his larger duty.

The Special Challenges of Blockade

For Nelson, doing one's duty was not only a matter of making difficult decisions in high-visibility situations, but was, at times, a matter of grinding hard work. This circumstance characterized Nelson's stretches of blockade duty, one of the lesser-understood applications of naval power. These important but often thankless assignments were wearing, frequently boring, and involved the risk of significant career damage if the enemy broke free from port. But naval blockade was one of the most effective military tactics applied by the British during their struggles with Napoleon, and no one was better at it than Nelson.

During most of 1804 and early 1805, for example, much of Nelson's time was devoted to blockading the French fleet in Toulon. Because of the high terrain around the harbor, which provided the blockaded force a better opportunity of observing the actions of the blockaders than the latter had to observe the activities of their adversaries in port, it was a particularly difficult assignment of its type. The challenge for Nelson was multiplied by the fact there were no nearby anchorages in which he could effect even minor repairs or replenish his ships.

Notwithstanding the challenges of the assignment, which tested the ships and their equipment and stressed the crews, Nelson was able to shape his blockade to serve both defensive and offensive purposes. By maintaining a close watch of the harbor with single ships and small units, he neutralized the French naval units and privateers at Toulon. In addition, by maintaining a system of communication between the ships on patrol off Toulon and his main force over the horizon, he eventually was able to lure the French fleet out of port and into decisive action with the Royal Navy.

Duty versus Personal Interests

Nelson's unyielding approach to duty also had considerable impact on his personal life. For example, in a letter to his wife-to-be in May of 1786, he lectured her: "Duty is the great business of a Sea-officer. All private considerations must give way to it, however painful it is."[35] Even in this major matter of the heart he felt compelled to make clear the order of things for a dedicated naval officer. This was to become a factor in the erosion of the relationship between Nelson and his wife, who seemed at times to see her husband's naval career as an inconvenience that kept them separated for long periods. Also, based on Nelson's aggressiveness, it was obvious that his career was a serious threat to her husband's life.

Lady Hamilton on the other hand was more in tune with Nelson's sense of duty and the basic requirements of his career. Her praise for his accomplishments was lavish to the extreme, and her position as the wife of a British ambassador made her more aware of military and political matters than Fanny was. As a result of Lady Hamilton's understanding of Nelson's powerful sense of duty, Nelson's love for her—although it seriously threatened to undermine his career—did more to enhance his performance of duty than to conflict with it. The striking exception was Nelson's official behavior in the Mediterranean after the Battle of the Nile.

Between December of 1798 and November of 1800 when he returned to Britain in the company of Lord and Lady Hamilton, Nelson concentrated his efforts in the Mediterranean on supporting the Kingdom of the Two Sicilies. His official behavior during this period, at times, crossed the line between aggressiveness and untoward harshness. And in some situations he openly disobeyed orders from his commander-in-chief in order to maintain his proximity to that kingdom.

Many believed that Nelson's primary motivation at the time was the fact that he had come under the influence of Lady Hamilton, the wife of Britain's ambassador to the Kingdom of the Two Sicilies. Even Nelson's strongest supporters among the British leadership— such as Admiral Sir John Jervis, Earl St. Vincent, who condoned Nelson's bold initiative at the Battle of Cape St. Vincent—saw Nelson's love interest not just an embarrassment but as an impediment to his performance of duty. And it was another of those supporters, First Lord of the Admiralty Earl Spencer, who finally ordered

Nelson back to England in 1800; there presumably he could, and in fact did, recapture his earlier perspective on duty.

Duty Under Fire

Nelson's initial combat experienced was as a teenager on HMS *Seahorse* off the coast of India. It was his first opportunity to witness the battle efficiency of a Royal Navy ship. From that first armed conflict until his death at Trafalgar, he fought in land battles from Sardinia to Nicaragua and sea battles from the harbor of Copenhagen to the anchorage of Aboukir in Egypt. He survived hand-to-hand combat and ferocious fleet actions; in the process, he faced death from cutlasses and cannonballs for thirty years.

Not unlike many who are noted for combat valor, he had little to say about the intimate details of his battle experiences. Most of his references to his personal battle experiences were clinical or pointedly dismissive. In his letters to his wife and other members of his family, he seemingly went out of his way to reassure them that even his most serious wounds were not worth discussing. After the loss of his arm at the Battle of Santa Cruz for example, he wrote to his wife that the wound really was not so bad and that, "my mind has long been made up to such an event."[36]

One notable exception to this self-effacing pattern occurred right after the Battle of Cape St. Vincent. In a series of self-serving letters designed to assure that his exploits during the Battle were made known, he wrote in considerable detail about his heroic personal actions while leading boarding parties to capture not one but two of the four Spanish ships taken that day. Over time, there has been criticism of that unvarnished boasting about his bravery. But perhaps it can be pardoned or at least understood in light of previous situations where his combat courage had not been recognized to the degree he thought appropriate.

Nelson's extraordinary ability to perform his duty under fire was not totally a matter of inherent bravery. The outstanding examples he had from those in the Royal Navy who served before him and with him played importantly. Although Nelson's performance in combat was considerably "above and beyond the call of duty," doing one's duty in combat had, by Nelson's time, become a tradition of the Royal Navy. Commanders from Drake to Nelson's contemporaries had routinely shown the way in battle. And if Nelson often appeared to be overly concerned about his own recognition, he also consistently recognized the example that had been set by his early commanding officers and commanders-in-chief. Nelson was part of a very strong tradition that had been built over hundreds of years, and he raised it to new levels.

Duty to the Forefront

As Nelson approached the climax of his career at Trafalgar there was a discernable shift in his personality. There was some falling away of the drive for honors and approbation that was apparent after the Battles of Cape St. Vincent, the Nile, and Copenhagen. By the time he was nearing the Battle of Trafalgar, he had achieved the status of Britain's leading naval combat leader, and he knew it.

He had suffered prolonged mental strain and physical stress in the process of achieving his unique status. And it was clear that both had taken their toll. Resignation to duty became a predominant theme of his letters as he pursued the French fleet across the Atlantic and back in the prelude to the Battle of Trafalgar. He wrote to his good friend and agent Alexander Davison: "But my health, or even my life must not come into consideration at this important crisis; for, however I may be called unfortunate, it never shall be said that I have been neglectful of my duty, or spared myself."[37] And it was that desire to do his duty—by then a quiet, fatalistic drive—which was a principal factor in pushing Nelson on to his final victory at Trafalgar.

Nourishing this deeply felt commitment to his duty was the British public's attitude, a force that bore him as on the crest of a wave through mental strain and physical suffering. That strong psychological support was never more powerful than on the occasion of the emotional send-off from the crowds that assembled as he left shore to go aboard the *Victory* for the last time. As he was being rowed to the ship, he turned to the *Victory's* captain, Thomas Hardy, and spoke with both perception and emotion: "I had their huzzas before—I have their hearts now!"[38]

His reception when reaching the fleet and meeting with his captains was equally emotional, and in another letter to Davison he wrote: "[M]y mind is calm, and I have only to think of destroying our inveterate foe."[39] In still another letter to Davison, Nelson provided a stark definition—one of many examples of his ability to capture a lot in a few words—of how he saw his duty at this point in his career: "I was called away, and I obeyed."

The Final Defining of Duty

From beginning to end, the Battle of Trafalgar added brilliant emphasis and sharp definition to Nelson's sense of duty. For example at the outset, as Nelson forged into battle and immortality, he ordered a signal, as he put it, "to amuse the fleet." The signal that he ordered, "England Expects That Every Man Will Do His Duty," graphically demonstrated his conviction that a primary requirement for each and every Briton as the battle was joined was to do his duty. That exhortation carried through the violence and confusion of the day, and now is one of the enduring pieces of the Nelson legend.[40] It was to be followed within hours by another Nelson reference to duty—his most dramatic of all.

During the battle, Nelson concerned himself with many things. He was worried that some of the British ships might have struck their colors; none did. He was concerned that the victory might not be the annihilation he knew was expected by his government; it was. He was concerned for the safety of *Victory's* captain; he survived. He was concerned about an impending storm; it struck with ferocity. And he worried about Lady Hamilton and their daughter, Horatia. But if his mind was occupied with all of those concerns, and more, during the combat, his last words as he died were both revealing and penetratingly simple. As he drew his last breaths deep below deck in *Victory*'s murky cockpit, he murmured: "Thank God I have done my duty."

Nelson ended his role on the stage of Trafalgar as he began it, focused on duty. As the battle began, his rallying cry about duty was emblazoned against the sky for all in his fleet to see. As it ended, the audience had changed, and Nelson spoke, in an almost inaudible voice, to a nation.

A dramatically understated plaque marks the place—deep below deck in HMS *Victory*—where Nelson died. During the several hours after he was wounded he expressed concern for the progress of the battle and the future welfare of Lady Hamilton and their daughter, Horatia. He also made the *Victory*'s captain, Thomas Hardy, promise to anchor as soon as the battle was ended; Nelson correctly anticipated a serious storm that struck after the battle.

Chapter 7

The Public Opinion Factor

"It settles everything. Some think it is the voice of God." That observation about the importance of public opinion was the colorful hyperbole of Mark Twain. Today Twain's homespun insight still resonates powerfully, helping us to focus on the relevance of public opinion to Nelson's career. Although Nelson didn't deal with our, "And now live from the battlefield . . .," media environment, and he probably couldn't even conceive of something like the Internet, it would be a mistake not to recognize the importance of public opinion to his career and the fact that he acknowledged its importance. The media channels of his time may have been more limited, but the weight of public opinion was still very much a factor for a combat leader of Nelson's stature.

The feelings of the British public about Nelson have remained overwhelmingly positive during the almost 200 years since his death—long past the point when military heroes usually recede into one of history's narrow niches. During his lifetime, these attitudes bore him, as on the crest of a wave, through mental travail and physical suffering. What made Nelson such an inordinately popular hero? In our contemporary social and political environment, which values popularity so highly, the answer to that question is particularly instructive.

Some Drawbacks

Before identifying some of the reasons for Nelson's phenomenal popularity, however, it must be noted that public opinion was not always his ally. In fact, there were a number of important public opinion factors working against his becoming the singular naval hero who finally evolved. Nelson's notorious extramarital affair with Lady Hamilton, which he flaunted, was an example of one of those negative factors. It made him seem foolish to many, including significant members of the press who cuttingly ridiculed him in print. In addition, his large ego and an accompanying craving for public recognition—reflected at numerous points in his career—also encouraged derision.

Even within the narrower confines of his professional deeds, notwithstanding their brilliant success, his actions were not universally applauded. For example his highly aggressive tactics in combat made him a potential threat to Royal Navy traditionalists and officers of lesser ability. His propensity for independent thinking and bold action—rising at times to a high-visibility departures from orders—were considered a threat to good discipline by many at the Admiralty. There his problems were compounded because of the way his love affair apparently clouded his professional judgment during his Mediterranean command following the Battle of the Nile.

Even his most loyal supporters among his fellow officers feared that his all-too-public extramarital affair would undermine his career. These supporters included Admiral Jervis, who was among those who most valued Nelson's strengths as a combat leader. In November of 1800, upon Nelson's return home from the Mediterranean in the company of his paramour, Jervis wrote to a colleague at the Admiralty:

"It is evident from Lord Nelson's letter to you on his landing that he is doubtful of the propriety of his conduct—I have no doubt he is pledged to getting Lady H received at James's and every where, and that he will get into much brouillerie about it."[41] Jervis's view was accurate and Nelson's disfavor among some at the Admiralty was duplicated at Whitehall and at Court.

Just how negative opinions of Nelson could be was demonstrated in situations such as a royal reception at which King George III publicly snubbed him. An army officer at the affair observed that Nelson was perceived "more like a Prince of the Opera than the Conqueror of the Nile."[42] Often opinions such as that were reflected in unflattering caricatures of Nelson and Lady Hamilton. However, whether he was oblivious to most of the criticism or simply indifferent to it, Nelson consistently defied disapproval from any and all sources. And in return for his enormously important victories at the Battles of the Nile, Copenhagen, and Trafalgar the British public—and, to a significant degree, its leaders in the Royal Navy and government—were willing to overlook the conspicuous flaws in his character.

In many ways Nelson didn't look or act the role of a conventional hero. He was of average height and during his early career he had an immature look that often masked his considerable command abilities. One army officer with whom Nelson served as a post-captain referred to him as "a light-haired boy." On first impression, Nelson was often perceived as shallow, as was the case when he first met the future Duke of Wellington, who was the eventual victor over Napoleon in the Continental land war. When Nelson learned to whom he was talking, his demeanor and conversation changed. From that point on, he was considered by the future duke as exceptionally perceptive.

Making him even less attractive physically, Nelson's appearance suffered from the ravages of tropical illnesses that he suffered early in his career. And afterwards as a result of combat wounds he lost his right arm and the sight of his right eye. He often was seasick and at the later stages of his career some said that he appeared prematurely old. Physically he had more the aspect of a military anti-hero than a hero. After his defeat and loss of his arm at the Battle of Santa Cruz in 1797, he reflected his own view of his physical condition in a letter to his commander-in-chief, Admiral Jervis. He wrote, "I am become a burthen to my friends and useless to my Country." And in the same letter, he requested a frigate "to convey the remains of my carcass to England."[43]

The Positive Side

Despite the many apparent negatives, Nelson benefited from predominantly positive public opinion, particularly towards the end of his career. Author Tom Pocock captured a special quality of Nelson's relationship with the public when he wrote that Nelson "was Superman with Everyman's weaknesses."[44] And this everyman aspect of the hero was doubtlessly one of the reasons the British public overlooked his controversial personal life and at times embarrassing ego. When crowds unhitched his carriage and pulled it through the streets themselves, and when battle-hardened sailors who served with him wept at hearing of his death, it was because he wasn't an ordinary hero. He was a hero who was neither above the people nor without common imperfections.

The highly charged, emotional quality of the public support he inspired was described by a young Yale College professor, Benjamin Silliman, who was visiting London in 1805. He could have been describing a present-day film or rock star: "Lord Nelson cannot appear in the streets without immediately collecting a retinue, which augments as he proceeds ... the air rings with huzzas .... He is a great favourite with all descriptions of people."[45]

Nelson himself apparently understood that not only was he a national hero but that, as Trafalgar approached, he had achieved a special connection with the public. And given Nelson's ego and need for praise, that realization must have been a significant contributor to his calmness and determination during the savage conflict to come.

In addition to Nelson's "everyman" quality, there was a very practical basis for his public popularity. Then Captain A. T. Mahan, an early and leading advocate of American sea power, put his finger on this particular factor in Nelson's public image in his 1897 biography, *The Life of Nelson.* In the preface of that work he identifies Nelson as, "the man for whom genius and opportunity worked together."[46] And it was the opportunity side of that equation that was the most important factor for Nelson's popularity with the British public of his time.

Nelson rose to senior command at a time when Napoleon was militarily dominating the European continent. This created the circumstances for Nelson to assume the role of a national champion in Britain's life-and-death struggle, not just for European preeminence but for the survival as a nation. None of the continental powers had been able to stop him. And as the geopolitical scales continued tilting in favor of the French, it was Nelson and the Royal Navy who stood between the British and European isolation, or worse, invasion and military subjugation. A recent analysis clearly describes the strongly personalized aspect of the rivalry. It says: "In this rivalry between land and sea powers, popular acclaim surrounded the two national champions. Their achievements seized the public imagination. Both Nelson and Napoleon became internationally known, the focus of media attention."[47] In this emotionally charged national life-and-death struggle, Nelson kept delivering what the British people— and the Admiralty, Whitehall and the Royal Court—desperately needed, morale-boosting victories.

This particular factor was also at least a part of the reason for his popularity in the fleet. The grinding hardships of blockade duty and the terror of battle were more tolerable when one could anticipate being on the winning side. And by the time Nelson had reached flag officer rank, his name in the fleet was synonymous with victory.

Not as obvious as Nelson's delivery of desperately needed victories, but still important to Nelson's public support, were some of Nelson's very positive personal qualities. For example he was a man of little guile. In an era when the practice of discreetly maintaining mistresses was widely accepted, he was blatant about his extramarital love affair. But his blatancy was not that of an iconoclast. Far from it, he was in many ways moral to the extreme. Everything in his actions with and writings about Lady Hamilton indicates that he thought their relationship was proper enough to be overt. Nelson convinced himself, correctly or incorrectly, that his relationship with Emma was literally a "marriage made in heaven,"even if not sanctioned on earth. And somehow he was able to rationalize his cruelly dismissive treatment of his wife, who remained loyal to him even after her public embarrassment created by their separation over a woman of questionable background. In December of 1801 almost a year after their separation, she wrote to Nelson: "Do, my dear husband, let us live together. I can never be happy until such an event takes place. I assure you again I have but one wish in the world, to please you."[48] The letter was rebuffed.

A Special Relationship

Also among Nelson's positive personal qualities was his concern for his officers and men—unusual for that time. As a result of this quality he inspired far more than respect and obedience. He inspired loyalty on an emotional level. In an era when such a punishment as flogging was common discipline for relatively minor infractions in the Royal Navy, Nelson, who judiciously tempered discipline with a recognition of good prior behavior and a record of steady performance of duty, forged an unusual relation with the lower deck.

It's hard to attribute that kind of sensitivity to a man who inflicted death and destruction so frequently and in such large measure in combat. Yet Nelson was visibly caring in a number of ways that enhanced both his public appeal and his effectiveness as a combat leader. In their Nelson biography, David and Steven Howarth focus on that quality: "He is remembered not mainly because he was . . . a great hero in the military sense—but because he was an exceptionally kind and lovable man."[49]

For many who fought with him, Nelson's concern for them was evidenced in the ultimate test of battle. Several combat incidents demonstrate this. One occurred when Nelson's arm was shattered during the assault on Santa Cruz, and he was being returned to his ship for medical attention. Although only semiconscious, he diverted the boat in order to pick up survivors from the sinking HMS *Fox.* The second incident occurred at the Battle of the Nile when he suffered an ugly head wound, and efforts were made to get quick attention by the surgeon for him. He protested saying, "I will take my turn with my brave fellows."[50] One can imagine the impact of that incident on the ship's crew, and how it was relayed mouth-to-mouth throughout the fleet. In a less dramatic but also important context, Nelson openly and frequently recognized that the fighting spirit and professional competence of his men were key elements in the Royal Navy's victories. If he was anxious for personal honors, he was equally active in securing appropriate recognition for those who fought with him.

One recent author paid special attention to Nelson's "unique strength of affection amid the ordinary seamen of the fleet, a society of men whose sentimentality could be as remarkable as their tough independence."[51] And a letter written by a seaman aboard HMS *Royal Sovereign* contains a simple and poignant description of how the battle-hardened men of Nelson's navy responded when they heard of his death: "Chaps that fought like the devil, sit down and cry like a wench."[52]

Another manifestation of Nelson's ability to personally relate to those around him was the strong and lasting friendships formed with many of his fellow officers, his "Band of Brothers." One member of this group of comrades in arms was Cuthbert Collingwood, whom he met early in his career, and who, as a vice admiral, led the column that paralleled Nelson's line of ships into battle at Trafalgar. Another example was his flag-captain at Trafalgar and later a vice admiral, Thomas Hardy, whom on one occasion he rescued from the sea under the nose of the enemy. It was another situation when Nelson's boldness gained him an advantage, and the enemy, who was startled at the aggressiveness of Nelson's rescue attempt, did nothing to prevent its completion.

It's fair to assume that there was a symbiotic link between Nelson's popularity afloat and ashore, and that the mutual support of both public opinion and loyalty among those who sailed with him undergirded his actions in combat, particularly those that were so risky to his life and career.

Self Help

Like many of history's most successful military leaders, Nelson paid considerable—some claimed inordinate—attention to his own image. Much of his self-promotion was accomplished through his letters and dispatches. His targeted writings that closely followed the Battle of Cape St. Vincent in 1797 are a good example of effective self-promotion. Although Nelson's commander-in-chief, Admiral Jervis, praised Nelson directly, his dispatches to the Admiralty describing the battle lacked the official recognition Nelson believed he deserved. Nelson corrected this perceived oversight himself by distributing a series of letters to friends captioned "A Few Remarks Relative to Myself in the *Captain*, in Which My Pendant Was Flying on the Most Glorious Valentine's Day, 1797."[53]

In the "few remarks," Nelson went into considerable detail about how he seized the initiative and turned out of the line-ahead formation to bring the British fleet into contact with the main body of Spanish ships. He also described his bold actions in capturing two Spanish ships-of-the-line by boarding the first from his badly dam-aged flagship, HMS *Captain*, and then crossing over the first captured ship to subdue the second. In several of his letters Nelson added a note that underscores an unerring instinct for effective self-promotion: "There is a saying in the Fleet too flattering for me to omit telling— viz., 'Nelson's Patent Bridge for boarding First-Rates,' alluding to my passing over an Enemy's 80-gun Ship."[54] The letters, thoughtfully dis-tributed, had the obviously desired ripple effect and Nelson's public reputation as a bold and successful naval commander was accelerated with the press and other influential groups. As a bonus, the phrase, "Nelson's Patent Bridge for Boarding First-Rates" was preserved for innumerable future biographers.

Nelson's efforts to enhance his own reputation through his written communications were magnified by his ability to turn a phrase under memorable circumstances. Many of those attributed quotes have been repeated in two hundred years worth of biographies and naval analyses. At times his way with words could be self-deprecating and based on black humor. An oft-cited example of this brand of humor occurred when he ignored his commander-in-chief's signal to withdraw during the height of the Battle of Copenhagen. When he was informed of the signal, he picked up his telescope, put it to his blind eye and remarked, "I have only one eye—I have the right to be blind sometimes . . . I really do not see the signal!"[55]

However, many of his most memorable phrases, both written and attributed, were much more than amusing or dramatically evocative; many were content-rich. One of the most outstanding examples of his ability to write both clearly and memorably is his Memorandum of 9 October 1805, sent to his captains before the Battle of Trafalgar. In this much-studied and quoted document Nelson analyzed the possible battle scenarios, outlined the tactics to be employed, and summarized it all in one of the most succinct combat doctrine statements ever written.

In a very different context, Nelson's last prayer written in the great cabin of *Victory* before the Battle of Trafalgar is an evocative expression of a warfighter about to enter combat. As expected he prayed for victory, but less expectedly he also prayed for humanity in the British fleet after the conflict was over. There also is a timeless quality to Nelson's last prayer, something that transcends politics, nationalism, and even fear of death. It movingly links many of the aspects of Nelson's combat character, including his relationship with God, his patriotism, his sense of duty, and his concern for the sailors of both sides whose lives were at risk.[56]

Critical Support

There is a seldom-discussed factor in Nelson's astonishing career that ultimately was as important as his popularity with the general public and those who served with him. Without the support of key military and civilian leaders—two special publics—he never would have had the opportunity for fame. The victories at the Nile, Copenhagen, and Trafalgar were made possible by the confidence of leaders such as Admiral Sir John Jervis, who was at various times Nelson's commander-in-chief and the First Lord of the Admiralty. In addition, Earl Spencer, who also served as First Lord of the Admiralty, and Lord Minto, a longtime friend of Nelson who served Whitehall in numerous diplomatic assignments, exerted important political leverage on Nelson's behalf. In Jervis's case, as a senior naval commander he saved Nelson's career after Nelson's defeat at Santa Cruz; he then continued to support him from senior positions at both the Admiralty and Whitehall. And it was Spencer who proposed that Nelson be put in command of the British fleet being reinserted into the Mediterranean in 1798, a first step towards the victory at the Battle of the Nile. Lord Minto's political influence also was a factor in Nelson being appointed to the Mediterranean command in 1798.

Both Jervis and Spencer had the courage to look past Nelson's faults and to put him in combat leadership positions that could have gone to other battle proven and less controversial admirals with whom the Royal Navy was blessed at that time. Cornwallis, Saumarez, and Smith are only a few examples of the many quality senior officers who were Nelson's contemporaries. However, in hindsight few would disagree that a safer approach would have almost surely denied Britain the series of unusually decisive and strategically pivotal naval victories achieved by Nelson. In the process, the decision-makers at Whitehall and the Admiralty left an important lesson for the learning: political correctness is not always the best criterion for picking warfighters who will win in combat.

The Reverse of the Coin

In addition to the impact of public opinion on Nelson, the long-term impact he had on it was and continues to be very important. British author, Brian Lavery, said it simply when discussing the Battle of Trafalgar in a recent book: "In some ways the legend of Trafalgar was greater than the reality but its long-term effect on public opinion and naval tradition was decisive."[57]

Nelson victories accelerated a broad-based public and political awareness of the potential of naval power in world affairs. His victories over Napoleon's navy were seen, with time, as arguably the most critical factor in the defeat of Napoleon's land power. The impact of that accelerated awareness reached well beyond Great Britain. It was reflected, for example, in the expansive reliance on naval power among numerous nations at the end of the nineteenth and beginning of the twentieth centuries. Those nations included the United States as it embarked—beginning with the Spanish-American War—on naval policies and strategies that were very different from those employed through the Civil War. Strategies based on coastal defense and commerce raiding were replaced by the global, more offensive use of naval forces that ultimately brought the United States to the position of the world's most powerful naval force.

The Nelson monument by John Flaxman in the transept at St. Paul's Cathedral is a departure from the highly idealized classical works of the time. Nelson is depicted in contemporary dress and the loss of the right arm and blind eye are evident. The inscription points out that the monument was "erected at the public expense."

The bow of HMS *Victory* projects the naval power she represented at the beginning of the nineteenth century. She was the flagship for Nelson at the Battle of Trafalgar and served in a similar role for other notable Royal Navy commanders-in-chief of the time. Today the ship—technically still in commission in the Royal Navy—is open for public tours at the Historic Dockyard, Portsmouth, England.

The Trafalgar Tavern on the Thames River in Greenwich, England is one of hundreds of pubs and inns in the United Kingdom that memorialize Nelson and his exploits. There is evidence that there was an inn in Lincoln-shire named after Nelson as far back as 1804. These "people's memorials" are an appropriate reminder of the "he's one of us" quality of his phenomenally durable public popularity.

The Board Room of the Old Admiralty has been preserved as it was in Nelson's time. It is believed that Grinling Gibbons did the elaborate limewood carvings surrounding the fireplace at the end of the seventeenth century. The wind dial over the mantle was a very functional item when even the best of naval plans was totally dependent on the direction and strength of the wind; it is still in good working order.

The Old Admiralty Building in the heart of London was the Royal Navy's nerve center in Nelson's time. Nelson, Jervis, Collingwood, and their colleagues passed through this arch to seek assignments to ships, make reports, and conduct other official business.

The London house on Bond Street—where Nelson lived in late 1797 to early 1798 while recovering from his wound at the Battle of Santa Cruz—still stands. From its windows, he watched the crowds that gathered below to cheer him. During his time at this house, Nelson was nursed back to health by his wife, Fanny. Many believe it was the time when their relationship was at its most positive.

The figurehead of Nelson from his namesake ship launched in 1814—the most powerful ever British ship-of-the-line—as it is displayed in the Australian National Maritime Museum, Sydney, Australia. It is evidence of the remarkable global reputation of Nelson.

The small silver plate in the foreground marks the place on HMS *Victory*'s quarter-deck where Nelson was fatally wounded by a French sharp-shooter.

Although urged to change the uniform coat that displayed his many decorations, Nelson refused. The fact that he was such a conspicuous target may have contributed to his death. In an unusual turn of events, it is claimed that it was the first time Nelson had appeared on deck in battle without his sword.

When Nelson was struck down on *Victory*'s quarterdeck, he was leading a fleet of men who made history. Despite his relatively young age, few believe he would have chosen other circumstances for the last day of his life. He fell doing his duty.

This ceremonial barge transported Nelson's body from Greenwich to White-hall, London, in January 1806 for Nelson's epic funeral. The barge is one of the exhibits at the Royal Naval Museum, Portsmouth, England.

Nelson's tomb is positioned directly under the Great Dome of St. Paul's Cathedral, London. Within the marble sarcophagus, Nelson's body was enclosed in a wooden casket made from the mainmast of the French flagship, *L'Orient*, which blew up at the Battle of the Nile.

3

Chapter 8

Battle of Cape St. Vincent

C ape St. Vincent, off Europe's mystical, most southwestern point, has been the arena for some of naval history's most dramatic events. In the fifteenth century, the cliffs that overlook the Cape were the site of Prince Henry the Navigator's school of navigation. In the sixteenth century, Sir Francis Drake mounted a daring and successful campaign against Spanish naval, merchant marine, and fishing ships in the Cape. And St. Valentines Day, 14 February 1797 was the occasion for another historic event at Cape St. Vincent—one that played a pivotal role in Nelson's career.

Double Importance

The Battle of Cape St. Vincent was important from two points of view. First Britain needed it strategically as a step towards turning the military tide that had been running against them in the Mediterranean and elsewhere in Europe. Second it was the high-visibility event that catapulted Nelson to national attention in Britain.

The previous year, Spain had been forced into an alliance with France, and that event made the Mediterranean untenable for the Royal Navy. As a result, Britain's naval forces were withdrawn from that strategically crucial region. By early 1797, Admiral Sir John Jervis—a tough disciplinarian and aggressive tactician—was in command of the British fleet operating in the area west of Gibraltar. The appearance of a Spanish force with 25 ships-of-the-line heading for Cadiz was an important opportunity for him to begin reversing the situation in the Mediterranean.

During the same period, Nelson had been steadily building his reputation while serving under Jervis—a well-executed single ship action leading to the capture of the French *Ça Ira* and the successful evacuation of Bastia, Corsica, were examples. He was a commodore embarked in the 74-gun HMS *Captain,* and his ship was one of 15 ships-of-the-line commanded by Jervis at the battle.

At that time, the odds were not unusual for the Royal Navy. And neither was Jervis's reaction, as his subordinates began counting the mounting number of Spanish ships. As his flag captain, Sir Robert Calder continued to count out the growing number of Spanish ships that were appearing, Jervis finally retorted: "Enough ... if there are fifty sail of the line, I will go through them."[58] It was to be Nelson's kind of battle.

Seizing the Moment

The Spanish fleet under the command of Admiral José de Córdoba was divided into two groups. As the approaching fleets drew closer, Córdoba's main battle unit of 18 ships-of-the-line was somewhat to the northwest of a group of merchantmen being convoyed by seven other Spanish ships-of-the-line. True to his word, Jervis formed the traditional line-ahead (single file) and split the two groups of enemy ships. However, at a critical point it seemed that the Spanish might escape Jervis's grasp as he completed a time-consuming maneuver requiring the British ships to turn in succession in their line-ahead formation.

Nelson in the *Captain* was the forth ship from the rear of the British line. He didn't wait to reach the required turning point. He made the most rapid turn possible given the wind direction, cut across the bow of the last ship in the British line, and headed directly for the Spanish ships. It was a bold and risky move, for which Nelson had no direct order from his commander-in-chief. And at one point, five Spanish ships simultaneously threatened the *Captain*. But the maneuver worked; Nelson joined the British van ship, HMS *Culloden*, engaging the rear of the Spanish force and throwing them off balance. The initiative at that point belonged to the British, and the type of melee in which the Royal Navy excelled was precipitated.

For many years, Nelson's turn out of the line has been described as disobedience to orders. However, a recent examination of the battle based on ship's logs and other evidence, suggests that it more accurately can be characterized as a bold and risky move that Nelson took on his own initiative.[59] Supporting that interpretation was the fact that Jervis had already ordered the rear of his formation to support the van as expeditiously as possible. However, no matter how it is labeled, Nelson's maneuver changed the course of the battle, a fact that Admiral Jervis readily admitted. In fact, when Captain Calder complained to Jervis that Nelson had acted without an order, Jervis's reply was blunt: "It certainly was so, and if ever you commit such a breach of your orders, I will forgive you also."[60]

From Ship-to-Ship to Hand-to-Hand

The next phase of the battle for Nelson was elemental hand-to-hand combat; it provided a drama that was to play exceedingly well with the public. In the process of Nelson's attack, the *Captain* was badly cut up. In fact, at one point the ship was so beleaguered that it was the intervention of Nelson's friend, Captain Cuthbert Collingwood in HMS *Excellent* that prevented the *Captain* from being overwhelmed. Notwithstanding the battered condition of the *Captain*, Nelson then seized an unforeseen opportunity, a tactic that he thrived upon in battle.

Two of the Spanish ships, the *San Nicolas* and the *San José* had run together in the chaos, and Nelson ordered his flag captain, Ralph Miller, to put the *Captain* alongside the *San Nicolas*. Nelson then led the boarding party that subdued the crew of the Spanish ship in hand-to-hand combat. Nelson's performance was notable on two counts. First, flag officers did not usually lead boarding parties, and in fact, Nelson had insisted on replacing Miller in that role. Second, Nelson had been badly bruised in the abdomen by a splinter—a particularly lethal form of crude shrapnel created by solid shot striking wooden ships during sea battles of the time—from a cannon ball striking close to him. Although the wound did not incapacitate Nelson during the fighting, it was to cause him ongoing physical problems later.

Having taken a bold action that was a tactical key to victory for the British and led the capture by boarding of one of the Spanish ships, Nelson had yet another feat to perform. After calling for some reinforcements from his own ship, he again led a boarding party, this time turning his attention to the *San José*. Again the opposition surrendered, and the *San José* became another personal victory for Nelson. The unusual means of crossing over one enemy ship to capture a second one gave rise to the colorful phrase: "Nelson's Patent Bridge for Boarding First Rates."

Showcasing Special Attributes

The Battle of Cape St. Vincent spotlighted a number of Nelson's most significant personal characteristics. His physical courage under fire, particularly the quality of that bravery, was one of the most important. Nelson did not simply overcome fear; he seemed to thrive on combat's perils. In fact, whether he was standing on the quarterdeck of a ship under enemy fire, or leading his men in hand-to-hand combat, he seemed energized and inspired by the danger. That quality had a powerful effect on the officers and men who observed first hand his conduct under fire. Inevitably, as accounts of his performance were passed throughout the fleet by word-of-mouth, it was the foundation for his legendary reputation within the Royal Navy.

Nelson's physical courage also was an essential part of his unparalleled popularity with the public. Brilliant tactics might be understood and appreciated at the Admiralty and Whitehall, but for the man in the street, courage under fire was what riveted his attention and, equally important, that of the press of the time.

Nelson's ability to grasp and act on a tactical situation was another characteristic vividly demonstrated at Cape St. Vincent. Two particular instances stood out. When he realized that only immediate action could precipitate the close-in battle, his commander-in-chief desired, he not only acted, he executed his move faultlessly. By "wearing ship" (turning away from the wind and direction of the enemy) he actually was able to get to his new course towards the Spanish van faster than if he executed the seemingly more direct, but more time-consuming, "tack" across the wind.

In his capture of the *San José*, he again seized a momentary opportunity. When he completed the capture of the *San Nicolas*, Nelson realized that he had an opportunity to board the second ship. Although under small-arms fire from the *San Nicolas*, he quickly regrouped and boarded the *San José*. Even he was surprised that the Spanish defenders surrendered quickly.

When the Battle ended, the Spanish had lost four ships-of-the-line to the British, and four others were knocked out of action. They suffered 200 killed and more than 1,200 wounded. The British lost no ships to the Spanish and suffered 73 killed and 227 wounded. The following day, the Spanish withdrew towards Cadiz, and the British proceeded to nearby Lagos, Portugal, for their repairs.

A Valuable Byproduct

One of the most important results of the Battle of Cape St. Vincent was the cementing of the relationship between Nelson and Admiral Jervis. For his part, Jervis had already shown a high regard for Nelson's ability, he had demonstrated this by assigning him duties in command of detached squadrons. For Nelson's part, he valued those opportunities highly, recognizing them as highly visible signs of confidence on the part of his senior. But more important, he saw them as opportunities for glory and advancement. As it turned out, Nelson was knighted for his exceptional performance at Cape St. Vincent. Jervis too was rewarded, in his case, he was named the Earl of St. Vincent.

Interestingly, although Jervis praised Nelson to his face and before his colleagues at Cape St. Vincent, he did not single him out in his official dispatches, which mentioned only Captain Calder, his flag captain. One can assume that he did not want to slight anyone when so many had truly contributed to the victory. In Jervis's own words: "The correct conduct of every officer and man in the squadron ... made it improper to distinguish one more than another in my public letter; because I am confident, that had those who were least in action been in the situation of the fortunate few, their behaviour would not have been less meritorious."[61] As events would show Nelson was able to overcome any possibility that his performance would not be widely recognized. And the mutually supportive relationship between Nelson and Jervis was to continue over the years—despite a later dispute over prize money—to the benefit of both men, the Royal Navy, and Britain.

Capturing Public Attention

Certainly one of the most important aspects of the Battle of Cape St. Vincent was Nelson's use of the event to gain public acclaim. It was not an easy task and not without controversy. For example, there was the jealousy of men like Calder, who did not understand Nelson's genius and resented both his success and the attention it generated. In addition, there were others who performed heroically at Cape St. Vincent—the "fortunate few" in Jervis's words—and many of those officers were Nelson's friends. In the face of those difficulties, two of Nelson's personal characteristics came to the fore and overrode the restraints. The first was his powerful hunger for glory, something that was evident in his character from the earliest stages of his career. The second was his instinctive understanding of the importance of public opinion in matters military. In the latter regard, he was similar to other preeminent modern military leaders who understood this fact of life.

Circumstances also played a role in the burst of public recognition of Nelson created by the Battle of Cape St. Vincent. Admiral Jervis's dispatch describing the events was sent back to Britain with Calder, who for obvious reasons wanted the dispatch he carried to be the sole news source for the battle. On his arrival back in Britain, Calder went to considerable pains to accomplish that end. However, the same ship that carried Calder and the dispatch carried two eyewitnesses to the Battle, Sir Gilbert Elliot and his aide, Colonel John Drinkwater. Neither was limited by Royal Navy constraints; both enlarged the public knowledge of the Battle to include Nelson's achievements. In Drinkwater's case, he had the additional benefit of a one-on-one post-battle debriefing by Nelson.

Timing was the final catalyst for Nelson's burst of fame. When news of the victory at Cape St. Vincent arrived back at London, Britain was in a state of crises. Fear of an invasion by the French was at a near-panic level. And in fact, the circumstances had precipitated a financial crisis. The reports of the events of February 14 filled a desperate need among the British population and government for good news about the war with France and Spain.

Pen Power

Nelson was both skilled and prolific as a writer. Those characteristics came to the fore after the victory at Cape St. Vincent in the series of letters labeled "A Few Remarks Relative to Myself in the *Captain*, in Which My Pendent Was Flying on the Most Glorious Valentine's Day, 1797." The letters were sent to people who could spread Nelson's account of his exploits, including but not limited to, the Duke of Clarence, his former commanding officer, William Locker—who was at that time the Lieutenant Governor of the Royal Hospital at Greenwich—and the Mayor of Norwich. The letter to Locker was particularly interesting in that it contained a note: "As I do not write for the press, there may be some parts of it which require the pruning knife, which I desire you to do without fear." There was no mistaking what Nelson hoped Locker would do with the letter. As it turned out, Locker obliged and the unabridged letter—which could be considered an early form of today's ubiquitous press release—became a piece of the legend-to-be.

Nelson's new national fame was not without cost. Many within the Royal Navy felt that, at the cost of his fellow officers at the Battle, he had gathered more attention than he deserved. However, significant momentum for the Nelson legend had been established; it would increase for the balance of his career, and survive for the two centuries that have followed.

Chapter 9

Battle of Santa Cruz

Nelson may have become a larger than life naval combat leader but he was not invincible. At the Battle of Santa Cruz, he led an attack on that city in Spain's Canary Islands that was a crushing defeat for the force he commanded. In fact the event in July of 1797 almost ended his career, and its study provides special insights—coming as they do from a rare Nelson defeat—into events that altered his character. In terms of history, Santa Cruz was a minor battle; in terms of Nelson's career it, was a defining point.

A Path to Disaster

Following the events at the Battle of Cape St. Vincent Nelson was knighted and hoisted his new rear admiral's flag aboard the 74-gun HMS *Theseus*. Operationally he continued to serve in the Mediterranean under Admiral Jervis, who had been elevated to the title of Earl of St. Vincent after the Battle of Cape St. Vincent. Nelson also had become a hero of some note in Britain and was given command of a small, independent squadron. In early July he undertook a bombardment of Cadiz that included a night action with Spanish gunboats. During the night boat action, he distinguished himself in hand-to-hand combat against the crew of a Spanish launch. The coxswain of Nelson's boat, John Sykes, twice saved his life during the action by deflecting saber blows. Sykes's action became part of the lore about the intense loyalty of those Nelson led, and the event added to his growing reputation as a fierce combat leader.

But an important by-product of the fame that came to Nelson from the Battle of Cape St. Vincent and his Cadiz successes was an apparent sense of invincibility. As he approached his first major detached fleet assignment as a rear admiral, his attitude—reflected in his personal and official correspondence—betrayed overconfidence. For example, he stated quite plainly that the praise he was receiving in the fleet right after the battle was in his own words "well deserved." That unfortunate attitude influenced Nelson's approach to the attack on Santa Cruz and his leadership during the battle itself.

Santa Cruz is the main harbor of the island of Tenerife, one of the larger Canary Islands. The harbor posed problems for any would-be attacker. It was backed by mountains and flanked by a rugged coastline. There were forts positioned to defend against attacks from either of the two approaches along the coastline. In their times, Drake, Hawkins, and Blake had all attacked the city, and Blake had achieved a notable success in 1657, destroying a sizable Spanish fleet there; however, Blake had benefited from an onshore wind during that earlier attack. Nelson recognized that, and he further realized that he could not rely on the benefit of similar weather conditions. Presumably that was a factor when Nelson proposed an assault plan in April that would not depend on ideal weather. This well-thought-out plan involved a combined Army-Navy operation that would have included several thousand British Army troops.

His initial plan proposed to Admiral Jervis contained Nelson's claims that the project "could not fail of success," and "the business could not miscarry."[62] Much of that confidence was no doubt created by the very successful combined operation Nelson led to capture the island of Capriai in September of 1796. The Capriai assault was one that Nelson conceived as a response to the barring—under French pressure—of British ships from Genoa, and it was carried out without bloodshed and in close cooperation with the Army. Nelson had initiated the assault, as a quick response to the Genoese exclusion of British ships from the port, without waiting for approval from his commander-in-chief, Admiral Jervis. As he had after the Battle of Cape St. Vincent, Jervis praised Nelson for his initiative in mounting the assault at Capriai. Again reinforcing Nelson's boldness.

However, Jervis was not able to secure the cooperation of the Army for the Santa Cruz operation. In June, when he realized that the Army participation in the attack was not forthcoming, Jervis asked Nelson if he was willing to try the venture as a strictly naval operation. Nelson, in a cocky response, said that with 200 extra Marines, and with "General Troubridge ashore and myself afloat, I am confident of success."[63] Troubridge, a long-time friend of Nelson's, at that time was captain of HMS *Culloden*, one of the ships-of-the-line in Nelson's squadron. The fact that two British frigates had successfully cut out the French frigate, *Mutine*, during an attack on Santa Cruz in May probably contributed further to Nelson's cockiness about the project.

On July 15, Nelson departed from the Mediterranean with a strong naval force of seven ships. In addition to the 74-gun HMS *Theseus* there was the 74-gun *Culloden*, the 74-gun *Zealous*, the 38-gun *Seahorse*, the 36-gun *Emerald*, the 32-gun *Terpsichore* and the 10-gun *Fox*. The 50-gun *Leander* joined the squadron after the initial, unsuccessful assaults on Santa Cruz and participated in the final stages of the battle. Nelson's orders from Jervis were typically general for the time, when basic communication could take weeks or even months. The immediate objective was to capture a Spanish treasure ship believed to be in Santa Cruz with a "sudden and vigorous assault," and to "take, burn, sink or otherwise destroy all enemy vessels of every description."[64]

En route to the Canary Islands, Nelson demonstrated his practice of briefing his captains on his thoughts concerning an impending battle and soliciting input from them. In fact they met four times during the transit. It was a practice that was to mark his leadership in future years. On July 22, the British arrived within sight of Tenerife's Mount Teide. Nelson intended to keep the larger ships *Theseus, Culloden,* and *Zealous* out of sight, while the smaller ships *Seahorse, Emerald, Terpsichore,* and *Fox* would work inshore under the cover of darkness. Nelson's plan depended heavily—in hindsight too heavily—on surprise to establish tactical momentum. The inshore ships would launch an assault on two forts to the northeast of Santa Cruz, where volcanic rock and heavy surf line the coast. Nelson intended for the frigates under Troubridge to disembark the roughly 1,000 strong assault force. He anticipated that this group would overrun the forts, and at dawn Nelson with the ships-of-the-line would enter the harbor and bombard the city's defenses. Nelson expected that the combined action would quickly cause the city's capitulation, and the surrender of the Spanish treasure believed to be aboard a ship in the harbor.

A Bad Beginning

The first problem when the British arrived was the wind, which was strong and offshore. As a result the boats loaded with the seamen and marines were still a mile from shore as dawn broke. "General" Troubridge returned to the *Theseus* to report to Nelson and to suggest that the assault force occupy the high ground behind the forts, rather than attempting to overrun them. That would, in Troubridge's estimation, achieve the same purpose as overwhelming the forts. Nelson agreed and the assault force was finally put ashore at about nine in the morning, at that point lacking the essential element of surprise.

The Spanish commander, General Antonio Gutiérrez—a tough and resourceful Castillian who had strengthened the Canary's defenses and reorganized the militia since his assignment there—quickly reinforced the position that was Troubridge's objective. After struggling over unexpectedly exhausting terrain in hammering heat and without adequate drinking water, Troubridge once again turned back. In the meantime the ships-of-the-line, faced with adverse winds and current, could not get closer than three miles. The operation was a shambles, and Nelson recalled the boats and inshore ships. The squadron then faced a new problem, a northeast gale with accompanying heavy seas. The squadron stood off and made the necessary preparations to ride out heavy weather that had set in. Two days later, Nelson was ready to mount yet another attack, but by that time, General Gutiérrez had an opportunity to further strengthen his defenses.

Some observers claimed in hindsight that Troubridge should have adapted to circumstances on the spot and pressed on with the initial assault, without returning to the *Theseus* for consultation with Nelson. By personally assuming leadership of the second effort, Nelson implied that he also held that opinion. After the battle he was explicit in voicing the opinion that, if he had been in charge of the initial assault, it would have succeeded. On the other hand—and very much to his credit—Nelson never openly laid the blame for the mission's lack of success on Troubridge's failure to adapt to the initial circumstances he faced. Nelson's avoidance of using a junior officer as a scapegoat for the failure of his mission was another quality that built great loyalty among his officers.

Some of Nelson's thoughts after the failure of his original plan were revealed in his after-action report to Jervis: "Thus foiled in my original plan, I considered it for the honour of our King and Country not to give over the attempt to possess ourselves of the Town, that our enemies might be convinced that there is nothing that Englishmen are not equal to."[65] However, he did not, as some have suggested, act impulsively, and in fact he continued to consult with his captains on next steps. By this point, realism, perhaps even pessimism, had set in. In a current book that sheds significant new light on the Battle of Santa Cruz, Colin White described the mood: "[E]veryone in the British squadron was well aware of the odds against them."[66] However, the arrival of the *Leander*, whose captain knew both the harbor and town of Santa Cruz well, added to Nelson's ability to plan in detail. The *Leander*'s arrival plus misleading intelligence—from a deserter from the town alleging great weakness and confusion among the Spanish defenders—might well have tipped the balance and led to the decision to mount yet another attack on July 24.

From Bad to Worse

Nelson's alternate assault plan was a version of the seagoing tactics he used later at the Battles of the Nile and Trafalgar: concentrate the attack, create confusion, and rely on the superior fighting skills of your own forces. But Santa Cruz was an amphibious assault not a sea battle. And his opponent, General Gutiérrez, was tough, experienced, and on his own ground. The failure to fully appreciate the exceptional ability of his opposing leader, who had only slightly more troops at his disposal than Nelson's assault force, was the second critical factor in the battle's outcome.

Nelson's lack of appreciation for the combat potential of the Spanish Army was based on his experiences with their Navy. This was reflected in a letter to Jervis several years earlier: "[T]heir fleet is ill-manned, and worse officered I fancy, and they are slow."[67] As Nelson biographer, Ernle Bradford, put it, "Nelson's experience of the Spaniards at sea had given him no good reason to respect them, but he had never encountered them ashore—except briefly in Nicaragua. He was unaware what magnificent fighting soldiers the Spaniards could be, and how—in those days—their colonial outposts were often manned by their best troops."[68]

The assault force, at this point reinforced by the *Leander*, was divided into several divisions. Nelson led the one that was to attack the enemy's central point by landing on the harbor's main jetty and then heading for the town square. Before disembarking the assault force at 11 P.M. on the 24th, Nelson anchored the squadron to the northeast of the city, making it appear that there would be another attack on the forts there. The diversion worked to the extent that Gutiérrez shifted troops from the town to the northeast. However, Gutiérrez's ability to quickly redeploy his regular Army troops and local militia from point to point during the battle negated Nelson's feint. The British never established the momentum needed to overcome a well-led force that was not inclined to panic, and that was fighting on familiar ground.

In the rough seas, the boats loaded with sailors and marines, who had to be exhausted, got fairly close to the shore before being seen. But then a murderous fire of antipersonnel grape and canister shot was unleashed. A small group including Nelson reached the mole, and surprisingly overwhelmed the closest defenders. However, they could get no farther in the face of the defenders positioned in depth around the jetty. And as Nelson was stepping ashore from his boat, his right elbow was shattered. The Spanish maintain that the wound was inflicted by grape shot, believed to have been fired by "El Tigre," a cannon that is today exhibited in Santa Cruz's Museo Militar, along with other artifacts from the battle. Current British accounts attribute the wound to a musket ball.

Many of the boats from the British ships were swamped and battered to pieces on the rocky shoreline or sunk by cannon fire. The *Fox* with about 180 of the assault force aboard was struck at the water-line and sank in the harbor. Nelson, who had been saved by the quick action of his stepson, Josiah, was evacuated to the *Theseus* in a commandeered boat. The semiconscious Nelson, in an action typical of those that endeared him to his men, diverted the boat to assist the *Fox*'s survivors. Once back alongside the *Theseus*, Nelson refused assistance and actually climbed aboard using only one arm. He immediately ordered that the surgeon prepare for the amputation that he knew was necessary—he was later to complain of the coldness of the surgeon's instruments. And in still another thoroughly implausible demonstration of his inner strength, he recovered almost immediately from the shock of his wound and the amputation of his arm. Based on his own account and those of others he was able to maintain his role as commander-in-chief of the operation from aboard the *Theseus*.

One small group of about 50 men led by captains Troubridge and Waller struggled ashore through the surf to the town's south. Somehow they fought their way into the town square expecting to rendezvous with other British elements that never were able to join them. At dawn, this group moved south and joined another small group, led by captains Hood and Miller, that was under heavy fire. Despite their small numbers, about 350, they set out to capture the town's citadel. However they were surrounded by disciplined Spanish troops, an effective militia, an unfriendly populace experienced at fighting off invading pirates, and even the remnants of the captured French frigate *Mutine*'s crew.

In a move that averted total disaster for the British, Troubridge sent a note under a flag of truce to Gutiérrez. The note threatened that the British would burn the town to the ground unless they were allowed to return to their ships. The British showed convincing signs of preparing to torch the town, and Gutiérrez agreed to the truce—perhaps as much in recognition of British audacity as in fear for the town. After a formal truce was signed, the remnants of the assault force returned to their ships with their military colors and their arms.

Aftermath

An example of the humanity towards the vanquished that sometimes emerges from the savagery of combat was demonstrated by the Spanish after the battle; it was later reciprocated by the British after Trafalgar. Gutiérrez and the town's inhabitants provided medical assistance for the British casualties and boats for their return to their ships. The town even helped to reprovision the British ships for their return to the Mediterranean. A Spanish description of the aftermath says: "[T]he generosity of the islanders under the direction of their commander overflowed. The Santa Cruz hospitals were opened for all the wounded, the soldiers from both factions fraternized, food and wine generously distributed and the Spanish ships returned the freed Englishmen to their fleet. The Tinerfeños' generosity moved Nelson to send Gutiérrez a modest gift of cheese and beer, along with a message of thanks for 'the humanity with which the wounded and all those who had disembarked were treated.'"[69] Gutiérrez reciprocated to Nelson's gift of beer with a gift of wine before the British departed.

Nelson reported the humane reaction of his adversary to Fanny: "[I]t is right I should notice the noble and generous conduct of Don Juan Antonio Gutiérrez the Spanish Governor. The moment the terms were agreed to he directed our wounded to be received into the hospitals and all our people to be supplied with the best provisions that could be procured and sent offers that the ships were at liberty to send on shore and purchase whatever refreshments they were in want of."[70]

The battle of Santa Cruz was not strategically noteworthy. It didn't discourage Spain who had reentered the war on Napoleon's side in 1796. It didn't change the strategic equation between Britain and France and, although it was a defeat for Nelson and there were serious British casualties, the British lost no ships-of-the-line. On the other hand the psychological impact on Nelson was important. His pride was checked. But thanks to Jervis, Nelson's spirit wasn't completely crushed.

Nelson's first dispatch—apparently the first full-length dispatch written left-handed—to Jervis after Santa Cruz was full of deep depression. By then the full impact of the defeat had sunk in—153 killed by the enemy, drowned or missing—and the process of burying the British dead had been carried out. The dispatch said in part, "When I leave your command, I become dead to the World; I go hence, and am no more seen."[71]

However, when Nelson rejoined Jervis off Cadiz on August 16, his commander-in-chief's greeting message struck the right chord. He assured Nelson that there was no blame to be parceled out, and that the attack had been attempted with "the greatest degree of heroism and perseverance that ever was exhibited."[72] Jervis had in fact reduced the fear of failure for his subordinate before the battle—and coincidentally provided a timeless verity for all leaders—when he wrote: "I am sure you will deserve success. To mortals is not given the power of commanding it."[73] Jervis, in a letter after the defeat, even demonstrated a note of grim humor, saying that on their meeting he would "bow to his stump," an allusion to Nelson's missing right arm, which was no longer there to render a salute to his senior. Jervis's handling of the situation reflected the comrade-in-arms relationship between the two naval officers and was one of many in which he was a positive factor at particularly critical points in Nelson's career.

Hard Lessons

There were important lessons for Nelson at the Battle of Santa Cruz. The first of these was that when an attack, particularly one based on the advantage of surprise, has begun there can be no hesitation. Troubridge hesitated at Santa Cruz, and surprise and momentum were lost. The Spanish forces were well prepared and by the time the second assault began Nelson had lost the initiative. That was a circumstance he would avoid in the future.

The second and clearly obvious lesson was that it is costly in combat to underestimate your enemy. Nelson had a thoroughly developed and viable plan to begin with, even without the Army force he proposed. A key variable that helped to tip the balance against him was the unanticipated competence and determination of his adversary, General Gutiérrez. Nothing in Nelson's or Jervis's writings before the operation indicates that they anticipated being up against such a tough adversary. As a result an experienced commander who prepared Santa Cruz's defenses well and maneuvered his forces effectively defeated Nelson.

But Nelson survived in body and sprit to fight another day. He returned to England; his wound eventually healed, and his self-confidence returned. Importantly there is no evidence that he ever allowed his determination and innate aggressiveness to swell into the kind of overconfidence that contributed to his defeat at Santa Cruz. His taste of defeat and humiliation there tempered him as a combat leader who was to grow to unparalleled dimensions.

Nelson's voyage back to England to recuperate was painful and his morale again sank to low levels. He continued to talk of his retirement, but in fact, he was soon to begin the most astonishing years of his career.

Chapter 10

Battle of the Nile

Trafalgar is Nelson's best known victory, but the case can be made that the Battle of the Nile in August of 1798 actually was more strategically important. In addition, the role of this battle in the ongoing development of Nelson's character as a combat commander was pivotal. It raised his status as a winning combat leader to an unprecedented level, further illuminated many of his leadership qualities, and set him on his final, seven-year course towards immortality.

Destiny's Path

For Nelson the prelude to the Battle of the Nile began with his return to duty in 1798, following his difficult, nearly yearlong, recuperation in England after the Battle of Santa Cruz. His return to duty came at another particularly critical juncture in the struggle between Britain and France. Napoleon had consistently defeated the European armies arrayed against him, including for the most part the British Army. In addition, Britain's allies—among them Austria,

Russia, Prussia, Spain, and Portugal—had steadily fallen away from the coalition that the British had formed against the French.

Counterbalancing Britain's strategic difficulties were a number of problems for France. Despite their successes on the ground on the Continent they had been prevented from carrying out plans for a direct invasion of Britain. That failure was based on their inability to establish sea control in the Channel, even for a limited period. Faced with the inability to mount a direct assault against England, Napoleon convinced the French Directory early in 1798 that a lethal blow could be struck against Britain by invading Egypt and then threatening Britain's East Indian possessions. As a consequence, the French Army positioned to invade England was disbanded, and an expeditionary force was formed to invade Egypt.

Against that geopolitical background the British government decided that the Mediterranean—an arena from which it had withdrawn the Royal Navy early in 1797, and in which it had no naval bases east of Gibraltar—was strategically crucial. Napoleon had taken advantage of the lack of British presence in the Mediterranean, and was known to be fitting out a major fleet in Toulon for a Mediterranean operation of considerable magnitude. The British were aware of the build-up, but they lacked knowledge of its specific objective. On 11 May 1798 the French fleet sailed from Toulon with Napoleon aboard the flagship *L'Orient,* where he spent much of his time with the large group of scholars that was accompanying him on the expedition to Egypt. The fleet gathered additional forces from Marseille, Civita Vecchia, Genoa, and Bastia. It ultimately included 400 transports and 35,000 troops for the forthcoming attack in Egypt. Finding that French Fleet and frustrating Napoleon's plan was a nasty problem for the British. Both Whitehall and the Admiralty agreed; Nelson was the man for the difficult assignment.[74]

A Big Stakes Sea Hunt

In March of 1798, Nelson had hoisted his rear admiral's flag aboard HMS *Vanguard,* and joined Admiral Jervis' fleet off Cadiz. In April,

Jervis placed Nelson in command of a detached squadron, the primary mission of which was to find and destroy the French invasion fleet with Napoleon embarked. However between May nineteenth and twenty-first, Nelson's squadron was pounded by an unusually heavy storm; the *Vanguard* was seriously damaged and had to be towed to the harbor at St. Pietro, Sardinia, for repairs. Nelson's reaction to the disaster—which had to be frustrating given the magnitude of his mission—was one of the clearest demonstrations of his confidence that God determined his fortunes. Equally important, it was evidence of a more mature attitude than the one he showed prior to the Battle of Santa Cruz. In a letter to Admiral Jervis he wrote: "I ought not to call what has happened to the *Vanguard* by the cold name of accident: I believe firmly, that it was the Almighty's goodness, to check my consummate vanity. I hope it has made me a better Officer, as I feel confident it has made me a better Man."[75]

It wasn't until 31 May that Nelson arrived on station off Toulon. By then Napoleon's invasion force was at sea, and there was little reliable intelligence as to its destination. It was a classic example of the chance intervention of nature in military events. Chance continued to play a major role in Nelson's mission as he just barely missed discovery of the French fleet on several occasions.

The bad luck and bad intelligence were compounded by Nelson's lack of frigates. This type of ship, frequently referred to as "the eyes of the fleet," was constantly in short supply for him. As a result he went through an extended period of extreme physical and mental strain. Noted naval author, Robert Gardiner, described the experience as "probably the most anxious and stressful of the great sailor's career, aware as he was that the fate of Europe might depend on his decisions."[76]

Several important facets of Nelson's character were crucial during the seven weeks he crisscrossed the Mediterranean searching for the French. One was his strategic comprehension and his willingness to make decisions based on it. That ability to keep his eye on the big picture matched his unique ability to grasp a tactical situation.

That long-view ability to see beyond the immediate situation eventually led Nelson to the conviction that the most likely destination of the French fleet was Egypt. In the end that strategic analysis was correct, and it paid big dividends for the British.

Other important aspects of Nelson's character came into play during his hunt for the French fleet. These qualities included his iron determination to maintain focus on his mission—notwithstanding circumstances that would have overwhelmed others. Despite the confusing reports and many frustrations—including the continuous lack of frigates for scouting and a lack of British bases for logistical support—Nelson pressed on in a murky situation. The lack of frigates became a near-obsession for Nelson during his stress, and he repeatedly complained about this crippling lack of a basic means of gathering meaningful intelligence. A typical reference to the problem was contained in a letter to Lord Hamilton written only days before the Battle of the Nile. He wrote: *"No frigates!*—to which has been, and may again, be attributed the loss of the French Fleet."[77] Even after the battle, lack of frigates was a problem. Nelson was eloquently emphatic when he wrote to Earl Spencer: "Was I to die this moment, 'Want of Frigates' would be found stamped on my heart."[78]

Still another aspect of Nelson's character illuminated during the grueling hunt before the Battle of the Nile was his willingness to risk his career to reach an important objective. He was rewarded when the enemy battle fleet was finally located in Aboukir Bay, 15 miles east of Alexandria. By then Nelson had missed his chance to strike at Napoleon and his army while they were embarked aboard their ships—something that probably would have ended Napoleon's career on the spot. But as it turned out an opportunity to at least short-circuit Napoleon's plans was still at hand, and he seized that opportunity with his characteristic initiative.

The Battle Begins

The French battle force at Aboukir consisted of 13 ships-of-the-line, four frigates, two brigs, and three bomb vessels. Their ships-of-the-line included nine 74-gun ships, three 80-gun vessels, and the immense 120-gun *L'Orient.* The 13 main force vessels were anchored in a line with the head of the line about one mile from shoals. The landward side was somewhat closer to shallow water, but as it turned out, not close enough. The French admiral, Brueys, presumed that the British would enter the bay in a traditional line-ahead formation, sail from the rear of the French line to the van, and bring the French ships under fire in sequence. Apparently Brueys also assumed that the British would not attack immediately, since sunset was approaching and night fleet actions were uncommon. He was wrong in both assumptions.

The British squadron also was made up of 13 ships-of-the-line all of 74 guns, plus a 50-gun fourth-rate ship, and a brig. Although there was numerical equality in terms of ships-of-the-line, the French had a number of significantly larger ships, and thus they outgunned the British. In addition, the British had to navigate without local pilots through unfamiliar waters with unmarked shoals— a challenge that many fleet commanders would have declined. Initially, the British squadron was not tightly formed up. Two of its ships were just returning from reconnoitering Alexandria harbor, and another quickly ran aground.

On the positive side and of particular significance, the British squadron needed no special preparation; their ships were ready for a variety of eventualities. For example they were rigged to deploy sheet anchors through the ships' sterns, which gave them additional maneuverability when the close-in combat began. Perhaps most importantly, Nelson's captains—his Band of Brothers—had been thoroughly rehearsed on a variety of possible tactical situations. Those situations included being confronted by a force anchored in a line in a strong defensive position. Nelson resorted to his "the boldest measures are the safest" principle and did the unexpected; he attacked immediately. As the battle was joined Nelson made only seven signals to his squadron, the last being "Engage The Enemy More Closely." This particular signal was to be seen flying again at the beginning of the Battle of Trafalgar.

Approximate Positions at the Beginning of the Battle of the Nile

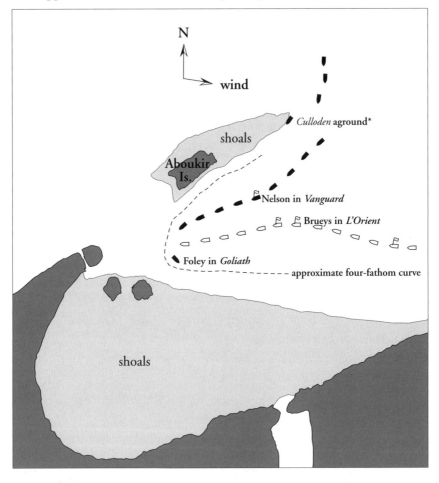

● British ships (13)   ◁ French ships (13)   ⚑ Admirals' flagships

* HMS *Culloden* ran aground before the battle and was never in the action.

Note: Drawing not to scale

As a result of his decision to attack immediately Nelson was able to exploit several weaknesses in the French situation. For one because the French assumed that there would not be an immediate attack, they had not cleared their decks completely. That failure hampered the gun crews' ability to serve their weapons efficiently. In addition, the French ships were anchored only by the bow and not closely enough to prevent the British from passing through their line. Lastly because Brueys did not believe the British would try to get between his line and the shoals, the French were not prepared to fight their ships to port. All of these advantages for the British were the direct result of Nelson's aggressive combat doctrine and practice of thoroughly briefing and rehearsing of scenarios with his captains.

The die was cast quickly as Captain Foley in HMS *Goliath*—possibly using a captured French chart—boldly crossed ahead of the French van, raking their lead ship as he did. Although it's debatable whether or not this specific move was part of Nelson's battle plan, there is no doubt that it was consistent with his doctrine that captains should seize the opportunities provided by circumstances. This frequently repeated willingness to rely on the individual initiative of his captains—another important aspect of his strengths as a combat leader—was vividly demonstrated at Aboukir.

Foley, after crossing ahead of the lead French ship, turned down the port side of the French line; he was followed by the second, third, and fifth ships of the British line, HMS *Zealous*, HMS *Orion*, and HMS *Theseus*. The fourth British ship, HMS *Audacious*, passed between the first and second French ships and then down the landward side of the French line. All four of those British ships then anchored in tactically advantageous positions and pressed their attacks. Coincidentally the ships that took up positions on the landward side of the French cut off support for Brueys from shore, where some of the French seamen had been caught by Nelson's quick attack.

The remaining weight of the British fleet, led by Nelson in HMS *Vanguard*, fell on the seaward side of the French van. Somewhat after the main British force attacked, HMS *Alexander* arrived from her scouting mission to Alexandria and passed between the seventh and eighth French ships, anchored, and entered the fighting with good effect. By then the entire forward half of the French line was under heavy attack from both sides, "doubled," by the British. As an added factor the direction of the wind was a significant advantage to Nelson. The French were anchored roughly west to east. The wind, a bit west of north, that carried Nelson into battle also prevented the rear of the French line from coming to the aid of its van. If nature had been cruel to Nelson at Santa Cruz, it was kind at Aboukir Bay.

The Dividends of Initiative

The fighting was intense, and British ships suffered serious damage. However the battle's outcome was not in doubt after the opening phase. Nelson had seized the initiative and never lost it—again in sharp contrast to Santa Cruz. In addition, the British gunnery, which emphasized up-close, rapid-fire smashing, rather than stand-off disabling, was superior in the tight circumstances and darkness in Aboukir Bay. Around 10 P.M., *L'Orient*, the imposing flagship and center of the French force blew up. The explosion was so momentous that for a period of time all fighting spontaneously ceased.

By morning the carnage had ended—one British seaman wrote that the entire bay was covered with bodies. The outcome was a stunning British victory. Although many of Nelson's ships were badly mauled and Nelson himself suffered a serious head wound, none of the British ships sank or struck its colors. On the other hand only two French ships-of-the-line and two frigates escaped, and Admiral Brueys was killed. As a postscript to the combat, all four of the French ships that survived the battle were lost to the British in later actions. Nelson's report to Admiral Jervis was the complete opposite from that following the Battle of Santa Cruz, and reflected the totality of the victory. It began, "Almighty God has blessed his Majesty's Arms in the late Battle, by a great Victory over the Fleet of the Enemy."[79] In a letter to his wife, Fanny, Nelson was equally unequivocal, if somewhat less formal: "Victory is certainly not a name strong enough for such a scene."[80]

War is often a matter of perception, and the reaction of the Comptroller-General of the French army in Egypt, expressed in a letter written after the battle, spoke volumes. He wrote in part: "The fatal engagement ruined all our hopes; it prevented us from receiving the remainder of the forces which were destined for us; it left the field free for the English . . . it was no longer possible for us to dream of giving the English an uneasiness in India."[81] Napoleon and his army had escaped destruction; his battle fleet had not. Just as his ambitions for conquest of Britain by a cross-Channel invasion was frustrated by the Royal Navy, so too was his alternate plan of striking a fatal blow through Britain's East Indies possessions.

The significance of Nelson's victory at the Nile was not lost on Britain's allies. In the Kingdom of the Two Sicilies for example, there was rejoicing that reached hysteria. Sir John Acton reported to Nelson from Naples: "[T]he stupendous news of the total destruction of the French Naval Force, at the Mouth of the Nile, by the brave and most energetic exertions of the Squadron under your command, has filled their Sicilian Majesties, and all their faithful Subjects, with the most sensible joy, gratitude, and extensive admiration."[82] The wife of one of Nelson's former commanders geographically expanded the sentiments: "All Europe has cause to bless the day you were born."[83]

Of greater importance than the celebrations was the fact that potential partners in a new coalition against France were influenced by the Royal Navy's resumption of control of the Mediterranean. And as another by-product, French positions in the Mediterranean became difficult if not impossible for them to support militarily. For example the French garrison at Malta—which had been occupied by Napoleon with minimal effort on his way to Egypt—was in time dislodged. Similarly French garrisons on the islands of Corfu and Minorca were replaced by British control. These shifts of control helped to relieve the lack of British bases that had hindered the Royal navy as it reentered the Mediterranean in 1798. Strategically Nelson's victory at Aboukir Bay was of historic proportions.

Aftermath

After the Battle of the Nile, Napoleon led the French Army of Egypt as far as Acre on the Bay of Haifa. There in 1799 his assault was repulsed and he was forced to return to Egypt. Not long after his failure at Acre, Napoleon realized that his Middle East ambitions were wrecked. He left his stranded army in Egypt and departed for France in August of 1799. He was, if not totally defeated, at least contained on the European Continent until his end at Waterloo.

Nelson's virtual annihilation of the French force at the Battle of the Nile had far-reaching effects on naval warfare, as well. It was an important step in the development of a new concept of combat at sea, one in which the total destruction of the enemy force was a realistic objective. Previously most sea battles tended to be fought to a point short of the total destruction of either of the combatants. It had only been in Nelson's time that sea battles had begun to be fought beyond the *bloody nose* stage. After the events of 1 August 1798 in Aboukir Bay there was a school of naval warfare that embraced the concept of total destruction of the enemy's fleet; that school's inspiration was Horatio Nelson.

In a geostrategic context the events in Aboukir Bay dramatically confirmed the fighting superiority of the Royal Navy at an historical juncture. On that basis the Royal Navy after the Battle of the Nile was confirmed as a prime force in British diplomacy by Whitehall and the rest of the world. For the next 100 years, no matter what the shifts in land power might be, there was little disagreement that Britannia ruled the waves. That fact of geopolitical life was to influence virtually every corner of the world for a century.

The Battle of the Nile had an equally significant impact on Nelson's character. Any doubts about his warfighting capabilities—his own or those of others—that might have existed after the Battle of Santa Cruz were blown sky high with the shattering explosion of *L'Orient* in Aboukir Bay. The battle's overwhelming results confirmed Nelson's status as a combat leader without equal; "The Hero of the Nile" was moving inexorably towards his later victories at Copenhagen and Trafalgar and towards immortality.

Chapter 11

Battle of Copenhagen

The Battle of Copenhagen revealed an intriguing dimension of Nelson's character, something that receives considerably less attention than many of his other qualities as a warfighter. That quality was his willingness—and somewhat surprisingly, his ability—to successfully negotiate an end to a major battle. This aspect of Nelson's personal make-up is particularly interesting in the light of his oft-demonstrated commitment to total victory in combat. The Battle of Copenhagen also reemphasized other qualities, displayed both before and after Copenhagen, that were keys to Nelson's combat leadership.

The events at Copenhagen in April of 1801 also displayed Nelson's character in a special way; they showed it in sharp contrast to Admiral Sir Hyde Parker, his commander-in-chief during the action. Hyde Parker was a very different kind of admiral than Nelson. He was a manager rather than a leader, and he was rich in prize money rather than fame. He was prone to caution rather than boldness, and he was limited in combat experience rather than battle hardened. He also showed little ability to inspire those he commanded. And in fact, he was known for practicing blatant favoritism among his officers.

A Time of Powerful Crosscurrents

In early 1801 there were powerful crosscurrents pulling at Nelson. In January he was promoted to vice admiral and became permanently separated from his wife. Also in January, he hoisted his new vice admiral's flag aboard HMS *San Josef* and was assigned to the Channel Fleet under Admiral Sir John Jervis. Within weeks he was reassigned to HMS *St. George* as part of a fleet destined for the Baltic and Copenhagen, commanded by Admiral Sir Hyde Parker. In February his and Lady Hamilton's daughter was born.

Also as the year began, there were significant political currents influencing Nelson's career. Addington had replaced Pitt as Prime Minister and Jervis, as the Earl of St. Vincent, became the First Lord of the Admiralty. The appointment of Jervis was particularly fortuitous since he was an experienced senior naval officer who was able to mitigate Hyde Parker's shortcomings and capitalize on Nelson's strengths.

Addington immediately began acting on the need to deal with a serious problem that centered on Denmark's shift towards an alliance with Russia, and presumably a closer alignment with France. Denmark traditionally had been a trading partner and political ally for Britain, and her movement towards a French-centered position was a serious threat.

Naval historian Nicholas Tracy described the situation: "Danish politicians were eager to appear well in the light of the rising French sun. They were committed to their new pro-Russian and pro-French alignment, and it was difficult in Copenhagen to appreciate that Danish policy was converting Briton into the most immediate danger of all."[84]

That growing shift of Denmark—and other Baltic nations that were united in the League of Armed Neutrality—away from

Britain and towards France had several crucial implications for Britain as a European power. And at that time, it was Britain's naval power that was its longest lever in the international power struggle.

First the changing political scene to Britain's north threatened its trade in that area which—although less important than East Indian and West Indian trade—was significant. Second the shifting politics to the north endangered Britain's prime source of naval matériel, something that was absolutely essential to its navy and merchant marine. Third the situation threatened what Britain considered the "legal regime of the sea," which was defined in British terms as the military and commercial freedom of the seas that enabled it to wield its sea power to advantage. Finally it was a serious setback for Britain's own alliance-building policy, one of the major means of containing France's growing power.

A Contrast in Personalities

Against this background Nelson found himself as second in command to a 61-year-old, wealthy and politically influential admiral who had demonstrated a very cautious approach to decision making and combat action. Prior to being assigned as commander-in-chief of the Baltic squadron being sent to Copenhagen, Hyde Parker had been in command of the Jamaica station. There he enhanced his reputation for magnifying his difficulties and slipping around responsibility. To make matters worse his commander-in-chief was showing little inclination to leave his new, 18-year-old bride— referred to as "Batter Pudding" in the fleet—to go to sea on a physically and politically risky mission. And as Hyde Parker's fleet was preparing at Great Yarmouth, it was all too clear to Nelson that the lack of good personal chemistry between himself and his commander-in-chief was going to be a problem. Somewhat surprisingly however, Nelson exhibited a degree of personal statesmanship and avoided a direct confrontation with Hyde Parker. That reaction to his new commander-in-chief was somewhat out of character, but it eventually worked to Nelson's advantage.

Instead of a direct confrontation or going over Parker's head to Jervis, Nelson chose to make Parker's inertia known to the Admiralty through his old friend, then Captain and later Admiral, Thomas Troubridge. At that time Troubridge was a Lord Commissioner at the Admiralty. Nelson's indirection worked; Jervis come down politely but firmly on Parker and succeeded in getting him and his fleet underway for the Baltic. Once underway the commander-in-chief kept Nelson in the dark about his plans, and what little Nelson did manage to learn displeased him. He wrote to Alexander Davison: "I have not yet seen my Commander-in-Chief, and have had no official communication whatever. All I have gathered of our first plans, I disapprove most exceedingly; honour may arise from them, good cannot."[85]

As usual Nelson was unalterably focused on the larger objectives of the Admiralty and Whitehall. Eventually, however, Nelson and Hyde Parker were to come to a reasonable working relationship, and the fleet arrived at Copenhagen during the night of March 30. By the time of their arrival, it was clear the ongoing negotiations with the Danes had failed and the battle was inevitable.

Nelson volunteered to take a portion of Hyde Parker's fleet and to attack the Danish defenses. After a council during which Nelson impatiently argued the case for his "the boldest measures are the safest" doctrine, Hyde Parker agreed to allow him to attack the main Danish defenses with a detached squadron. Accounts of the debate in the council emphasized one of Nelson's most important qualities and a side of his personality that had been building steadily. During the discussions, Nelson's ability to energize the situation with a powerful combination of aggressiveness, confidence, and persuasiveness was very much a factor in the decisions that were made.

Situation Analysis

The Danes had a strong defensive position and Parker's cautious approach to the battle had given them a chance to continue strengthening their defenses right up to the last moment. However, Crown

Prince Frederick chose to command directly all of the Danish defenses, both the shore batteries and afloat units, which turned out to be a weakness that played into Nelson's strengths. Because there was no single Danish naval commander afloat, Nelson's bold tactics were particularly effective.

There were some tactical similarities at Copenhagen with the situation Nelson had faced at Aboukir Bay. The portion of the Danish force that Nelson planned to attack was anchored in a line, and as Admiral Brueys had done before the Battle of the Nile, the Danes did not provide an ability to maneuver their ships at anchor with the use of spring lines. This failure limited the arc of fire of each Danish unit in the line. As a result—and despite the very restricted area of the action—Nelson had the advantage of at least some maneuverability as his ships faced off with a rigid line of defense. In addition, he ordered his captains to be prepared to anchor by the stern and to use spring lines to maneuver their anchored ships into advantageous firing positions. On the other hand, unlike the French at Aboukir Bay, the Danes were able to support their line of ships and floating batteries from the shore, and they did so with effect.

The Danish line was made up of a variety of ships and floating gun platforms anchored with shoal waters and the city of Copenhagen on one side of their line and a fairly narrow channel on the other. At the north end of the Danes' position were two small islands, Crown and Little Crown, with significant batteries. There also was a battery at Amager Island to support the south end of the Danish line, and yet another battery to support the north end at Trekroner Fort. The Danes had 19 ships and floating gun platforms in their line and Nelson's squadron started with 10 ships-of-the-line, two 50-gun ships, five frigates, two sloops, and seven bomb vessels.

Nelson mounted his attack with 17 ships and—when the Crown, Little Crown, Amager, and Trekroner batteries were calculated—he faced a formidable challenge. In another similarity to the Battle of the Nile, the enemy made an incorrect initial assumption; they expected the attack to come from the opposite direction than

Approximate Positions during the Battle of Copenhagen

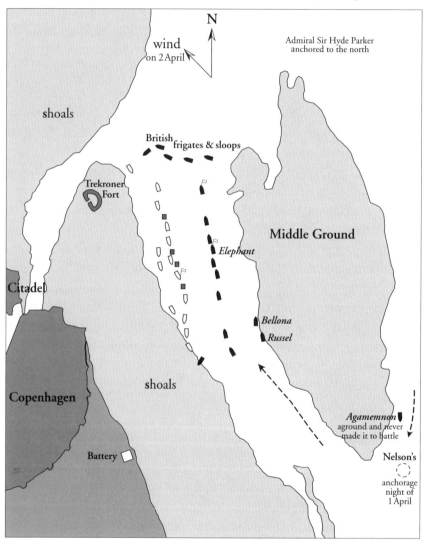

N

wind
on 2 April

Admiral Sir Hyde Parker
anchored to the north

shoals

British frigates & sloops

Trekroner Fort

Middle Ground

Elephant

Citadel

Bellona
Russel

shoals

Copenhagen

Agamemnon
aground and never
made it to battle

Battery

Nelson's

anchorage
night of
1 April

- British ships (12)   ⚑ Admiral's flag ship
- ◁ Danish ships (14)   ■ Danish Floating Batteries (4)
- ◄----- Nelson's course April 1 and 2

Note: Drawing not to scale

that chosen by Nelson. In this case the Danes assumed that the British attack would come from the north. However Nelson did the unexpected by overcoming difficult navigational circumstances and moving his squadron into position to attack from the south.

In yet one more similarity with a previous battle, the direction of the wind was a crucial factor. At the Battle of Santa Cruz the offshore winds thwarted Nelson's plans for a surprise attack and contributed to his defeat. At Copenhagen Nelson needed a north wind to carry his ships past a large shoal area called the Middle Ground and then a south wind to allow him to come back into the deep water inside the Middle Ground where the Danish line was anchored. From that direction, he was able to do the unexpected and sail from the south to the north of the Danish line. At 2:30 P.M. on the first of April, with the wind from the north, he signaled for his squadron to set sail. By nightfall his ships were anchored in position for the following day's attack. On the morning of April 2, between 9:30 and 10:00 A.M., with the wind now out of the southeast, Nelson signaled for the British squadron to weigh anchor in succession; the struggle was about to begin. Once again nature had cooperated with Nelson's boldness.

A Slugging Match

During the early phase of the battle, HMS *Agamemnon* was unable to get around the southern tip of the Middle Ground and never did get into action; it was the first price Nelson paid for his decision to attack from the south. Two other ships, HMS *Russell* and HMS *Bellona* went aground on the western edge of the Middle Ground and played a reduced role in the fighting, another price paid for Nelson's boldness. And, HMS *Elephant* nearly went aground on the western edge with Nelson aboard. Had his seaman's judgement not led him to ignore his pilot's directions, a disastrous grounding for the flagship would have occurred.

Nelson's squadron pressed on and carried out his basic tactical plan, which was to concentrate as much damage as possible to the enemy's ships at the southern end of the Danish line and then match up with their entire line. A lethal slugging match followed, during which both sides fought bravely. Despite the Danes' tenacity, the advantage eventually began to tilt towards the British. As the afternoon wore on the battle's outcome became clear. And at 3:30 when a flag of truce was hoisted aboard the *Elephant* only two Danish units, a ship-of-the-line and a floating gun battery, were still fighting. And both of those units were being hard pressed. During the battle none of Nelson's ships, other than the *Agamemnon,* were out of action, although there was heavy damage to several of them.

During the height of the combat there was an incident that vividly revealed Nelson's willingness to ignore an order that was not consistent with a primary objective. At 1:30 in the afternoon Admiral Hyde Parker—who was observing the chaotic battle from his flagship to the north—sent a general signal to Nelson's squadron to "Discontinue The Action." Because it was a general signal from the commander-in-chief, every ship in Nelson's squadron was required immediately to break off action. But, to do so would have converted what was becoming a hard-fought British victory into a costly defeat.

Fortunately most of the ships followed Nelson's lead, ignored the order, and fought on to victory. Only a few of the smaller British ships—those that were too close to the commander-in-chief to ignore the signal—responded to it. It was a classic example of Nelson being willing, based on his own first-hand knowledge, to depart from an order from a superior who was not familiar with the immediate situation.

The incident not only became another of Nelson's famous departures from orders, it coincidentally demonstrated the strong bond between Nelson and his captains, who chose to follow his example rather than a general order from Admiral Hyde Parker. The incident also enhanced Nelson's reputation for black humor—particularly under fire—when he referred to his right "to be blind sometimes" when he was told of Admiral Hyde Parker's signal. It was typical Nelson, the stuff of legends.

A Reluctant Diplomat

Although the victory clearly was Britain's, the combat was halted— at Nelson's initiative—while both the Danes and the British had portions of their fleets that were not committed to the struggle. In both his first and second truce messages Nelson cited "humanity" as his motivation for the truce. It's also likely that Nelson saw a better opportunity to reestablish close relations with the Danes if they were not completely crushed and Copenhagen battered. Nelson knew that the reestablishing of a strong relationship between the Danes and the British would undercut the League of Armed Neutrality and facilitate the elimination of Russia as a potential French ally and British opponent. He was, as usual, focused on strategic objectives beyond victory for its own sake.

After the combat of April 2 and the truce negotiated by Nelson, Hyde Parker, as commander-in-chief, reentered the picture as Britain's senior representative and primary negotiator. He immediately reverted to the original terms that had been rejected by the Danes. During the following days Nelson was an integral part of the negotiation process, and it was clear that his reputation as a courageous and blunt-speaking combat leader brought credibility to the negotiations that Hyde Parker lacked. Nelson's continued references to the traditional friendship between Danes and Britons, combined with periodic threats that included allusions to the destruction of Copenhagen, were effective. The final result was an armistice that worked to the benefit of Britain and again demonstrated Nelson's ability to recognize the larger objectives of the Royal Navy and Britain.

After the battle Nelson explained the rationale for his truce proposal in a letter to the Prime Minister. He wrote to Addington: "[T]he moment of a complete victory was surely the proper time to make an opening with the Nation we had been fighting with."[86] This was a strikingly different approach to the battle than the one he had reflected towards the French at the Battle of the Nile, or the attitude later reflected at Trafalgar. And as turned out, Nelson's willingness to negotiate an end to the conflict paid diplomatic dividends for the British government.

A Footnote to the Battle

After the battle Hyde Parker, not unexpectedly, rewarded those who were politically close to him, many of whom were not directly involved in the actual combat. In the process he bypassed many who had actually fought with great courage. In doing so, he negated a once-in-a-lifetime opportunity for a key promotion for officers who had showed courage and skill under fire.

Hyde Parker's cronyism was so flagrant that Nelson took it upon himself to fight with the Admiralty and Whitehall for the deserved promotions and honors for those who had born the brunt of combat at Copenhagen. As is often the case when corridor politics are pitted against combat valor, the former seemed to a large extent to have prevailed. However, Nelson's willingness to risk his own standing to gain recognition for those who really deserved it was another strong reason for the uncommon loyalty of his subordinates.

Notwithstanding Nelson's contentiousness with officialdom, Hyde Parker's flaws finally outweighed his political leverage, and—with a confrontation with Russia next at hand—he was replaced by Nelson as commander-in-chief in the Baltic. One of the officers wrote about the reaction in the fleet when Nelson made his first signal as commander-in-chief of the fleet: "The fleet to hoist in all boats and prepare to weigh." He wrote: "This at once showed how different a system was about to be pursued; it having been intended that the Fleet should await at anchor fresh instructions from England." At a later point, the letter continued: "The joy with which the signal was received not only manifested what are the customary feelings on those occasions, but was intended as peculiarly complimentary to the Admiral."[87]

As events—including the death of Czar Paul—rapidly developed after the Battle of Copenhagen, the League of Armed Neutrality broke up and made further action by Nelson against Russia and Sweden unnecessary. In July of 1801, Nelson was back in Britain. At this point only one more major battle awaited Nelson.

Chapter 12

Battle of Trafalgar

B ritish author Oliver Warner, who wrote authoritatively about the Battles of the Nile and Trafalgar, said that Trafalgar was "different from and more conclusive than any earlier battle under sail."[88] Another well-known Nelson author, Dudley Pope, described the savage battle that occurred off Cape Trafalgar on October 21, 1805, and the events that led up to it, simply as, "the most famous naval campaign and battle in history."[89]

Whatever else that climactic struggle south of Cadiz was, it also was the most dramatic demonstration of how Nelson's unique qualities as a warfighter came together in the ultimate test of battle. Trafalgar brilliantly illuminated the total impact of Nelson's personality as a powerful force multiplier, a phenomenon that propelled the Royal Navy to a series of history-shaping naval victories.

Part of a Bigger Picture

Trafalgar was the culmination of a multifaceted British maritime strategy to contain and eventually defeat Napoleon, who at one point referred to the British as "these tyrants of the seas." It was, according to one recent description, "the story not just of the morning and afternoon in which Nelson ... smashed the combined fleets of France and Spain, but also that of a complex campaign of which Trafalgar was the climax."[90] That campaign was the broad path that led Nelson to his final combat victory and lasting fame.

A convenient historical entry point for examining the events leading up to Trafalgar is the renewal by Britain in April of 1803 of its ongoing war with France. That renewal had been anticipated by the British government with a naval rebuilding effort that resulted in 75 ships-of-the-line being in service by the end of 1803. Thus Britain entered the renewed war with a powerful naval nucleus around which they continued to build.

In contrast—and because the renewal of war came before Napoleon anticipated it—the numbers of French ships-of-the-line in service or under construction in May of that year were 47 and 19 respectively.[91] And despite further ship building, Napoleon's navy was never able to escape its strategic inferiority to the Royal Navy— even when later augmented by the addition of the Spanish fleet when that country became an ally of France in December of 1804. In simple terms the Royal Navy was an extremely effective instrument of British power, while Napoleon's navy was considerably less important in regard to his international affairs. One of the clearest reflections of this was that the French navy never achieved the superior numbers and proficiency required to seize control of the English Channel, even for a limited period, for an all-out invasion of Britain.

At the renewal of war in 1803 there also were significant differences in how the British and French employed their naval forces. Napoleon always viewed his navy from the perspective of an army general, and primarily in relation to his land campaigns. In particular, when all was said and done, Napoleon saw his navy as an enabler for the invasion of Britain by the French Army. In contrast the British government perceived the Royal Navy as—in the words of one contemporary author—"the main weapon by which Britain waged war."[92] This made Nelson's emergence as the Royal Navy's preeminent senior warfighter of momentous historical importance.

The British naval capability was built around two main fleets. One of these, the Ushant fleet, was responsible for a variety of missions, which included the protection of Britain against a French invasion, protection of British merchantmen in the Channel area, and the suppression of French naval forces and privateers operating out of Brest, Cherbourg, and other French Atlantic ports.

The other main fleet operated in the Mediterranean and had a wide range of responsibilities. Among the missions of that fleet were the suppression of the French naval units and privateers in the theater, protecting such allies as the Kingdom of the Two Sicilies, convoying merchant ships, and dealing with diplomatic and military irritants like the Dey of Algiers. Of paramount importance were the objectives of blocking France's military ambitions on the central and eastern Mediterranean rim and facilitating an alliance with Russia and others against Napoleon. Special squadrons were formed to cover such strategic areas as the West Indies and the Irish coast, and units were detached from or joined with the two main fleets as circumstances required.

The result of this sea-based strategy was that the Royal Navy was constantly on the move. Its duties were arduous and stretched crews and materiel to their limits. But as a positive consequence, the British crews were well trained and confident. For them combat was a release, and Nelson epitomized and accelerated this offensive predisposition. He frequently reflected his attitude with acerbic statements, such as his assessment of the French fleet blockaded in Cadiz before the Battle of Trafalgar: "These gentlemen must soon be so perfect in theory, that they will come to sea to put their knowledge into practice."[93] In contrast, the French crews, although courageous, were neither honed nor hardened to the high degree of the Royal Navy. And the purging of much of the French Navy's professional officer corps during the French Revolution seriously compounded the problem for Napoleon's navy. This latter circumstance provides a noteworthy example of how the application of political correctness, as a selection criterion for success among its leadership, undercuts the potency of a fighting force.

Nelson Enters the Mediterranean

In May of 1803, Nelson was appointed commander-in-chief of Britain's Mediterranean fleet. He had 14 years of wartime experience against the French, and he was tireless, aggressive, and totally dedicated to maintaining his forces in a constant state of readiness. He also knew the operating area intimately, having previously been commander-in-chief of a British squadron returned to the Mediterranean in 1798.

For months Nelson doggedly took care of business in the Mediterranean. Despite his own deteriorating health—he repeatedly wrote of retirement and rest—he paid close attention to the health of his sailors and the readiness of his ships. One of the more significant characteristics of his command was the special quality of Nelson's blockade of the French fleet in Toulon. He used his forces to closely monitor the enemy rather than to block their exit with a powerful, on-site fleet. His tactic was to neutralize the French naval force, with the ultimate objective to lure them out of port and totally destroy them. In his own characterization of his methods he said, "[T]he Port of Toulon has never been blockaded by me: quite the reverse—every opportunity has been offered the Enemy to put to sea, for it is there that we hope to realize the hopes and expectations of our Country."[94]

In January of 1805 Nelson's blockade tactic worked. The French fleet led by Admiral Villeneuve sortied from Toulon only to be driven back into port by a storm. However Villeneuve once again broke out on March 30, and that time he was not driven back by the weather. Unfortunately the second part of Nelson's planned scenario—the all-out engagement between the British and French—didn't occur. Weather favorable to Villeneuve, a lack of reliable British intelligence, and an insufficient number of frigates for scouting—

the latter two reminiscent of the prelude to the Battle of the Nile—allowed Villeneuve to slip out of the Mediterranean and head for the West Indies.

Napoleon's strategy at this point was for Villeneuve's force to attack British colonies in the West Indies and then join with another fleet on a similar mission there. The two combined fleets would then return to the English Channel. Once back in the Channel area, the combined force from the West Indies would join additional French ships and cover an invasion of the English coast. With interesting symmetry, the first parts of both Nelson's blockade strategy and Napoleon's invasion strategy worked, and in each case the second parts failed. Villeneuve escaped Toulon and avoided Nelson. However after a brief period of ineffective operations in the West Indies, he failed to effect the union with other French naval forces intended by Napoleon.

Villeneuve's breakout from Toulon and subsequent departure for the West Indies were a severe physical and mental test for Nelson. After weeks of searching to determine where Villeneuve was heading—Nelson was wrongly convinced the French fleet's destination was Alexandria—it was confirmed that it had cleared Gibraltar heading towards the West Indies. Nelson left Lagos, Portugal on 11 May, roughly a month behind his adversary, and headed west across the Atlantic in pursuit.

Nelson's pursuit of the fleet from Toulon again demonstrated at least two elements of his leadership that were—by the time of Trafalgar—deeply ingrained in his character. One was his ability to perceive the larger objectives of Britain's maritime strategy, and the second was his dogged determination to carry out the missions he knew were consistent with that strategy. This latter quality also had been demonstrated on previous occasions, such as his months-long, nerve-racking hunt for French Admiral Brueys's fleet leading up to the Battle of the Nile in 1798. At the Battle of Copenhagen in 1801 both qualities were in play as his fierce determination, even when confronted with a defensive position that would have deterred most commanders, reflected his appreciation of the importance of preventing the Baltic countries from increasing their cooperation with Napoleon.

Nelson's decision to pursue Villeneuve across the Atlantic also represented another noteworthy example of his willingness to risk his career by making difficult decisions. There was nothing in Nelson's orders that told him to pursue the French to the West Indies. But in evaluating all of the factors, with his usual grasp of strategy beyond his immediate sphere, he determined that a victory over Villeneuve in the West Indies would be as significant as one in the Mediterranean.

If Villeneuve had succeeded in effecting the grand union planned by Napoleon while Nelson trailed behind him, Nelson probably would have been blamed for a British military disaster and disgraced. Fortunately for the British and for Nelson, his arrival in the West Indies cut short Villeneuve's ability to do mischief there and kept events moving towards Trafalgar.

Overture to Battle

On 22 July 1805, as he was returning to Europe from the West Indies, Villeneuve encountered a British squadron commanded by Vice Admiral Sir Robert Calder. The results of the battle were inconclusive, and the French fleet took refuge in Cadiz, which the British promptly blockaded. But, Villeneuve's brush with Calder revealed the disposition and expectations of the Admiralty. They promptly court-marshaled and censured Calder for not achieving a conclusive victory, despite the fact that many thought he had done as well as could be expected. The reaction of the Admiralty showed that there was complete agreement among the Admiralty, Whitehall, and Nelson: major units of the French fleet must be annihilated at every opportunity. Nelson phrased it clearly in a letter to the Admiralty: "[I]t is, as Mr. Pitt knows, annihilation that the Country wants."[95] Nelson clearly understood that stand-offs or marginal successes did not advance the British maritime strategy.

On 19 August, Nelson arrived back in England for a brief respite. He had not set foot ashore since June of 1803, and he was completely exhausted. He headed for Merton, the home he had established with Lady Hamilton, and began a long-overdue leave. The stage was set for the Battle of Trafalgar.

Opening Phase

On 28 September, Nelson rejoined the British fleet off Cadiz. He described the reaction, which reflected the unusual bond between him and his Band of Brothers: "The reception I met with on joining the Fleet caused the sweetest sensation of my life. The Officers who came on board to welcome my return, forgot my rank as Commander-in-Chief in the enthusiasm with which they greeted me."[96] He had 29 ships-of-the-line, six of which were due for resupply, and found 36 ships-of-the-line in the combined French-Spanish fleet in Cadiz. Notwithstanding this significant numerical disadvantage, his reaction was typical Nelson: "I am not come forth to find difficulties, but to remove them."[97] During the following weeks, Nelson rotated ships into Gibraltar for water and other replenishing. He also found opportunities to communicate with his friend of many years and second in command, Vice Admiral Collingwood, and his captains, to inform them of his intentions concerning bringing the combined fleets of France and Spain to action.

The most noteworthy of his written communications was his secret Memorandum of 9 October 1805.[98] In this plan of attack Nelson outlined his tactics in general terms. The Memorandum is more a confirmation of a winning combat doctrine than a precise plan of attack—a point too often lost in the analyses of the Battle of Trafalgar. Nelson's own words suggest this: "Something must be left to chance; nothing is sure in a Sea Fight." Later he sums up everything in one sentence that is arguably the best expression of a naval combat doctrine ever written: "But, in case Signals can neither be seen or perfectly understood, no Captain can do very wrong if he places his Ship alongside that of an Enemy." In a few words Nelson clearly established the basic combat guidelines for his captains and for Admiral Collingwood; and the earlier super-confidence he showed before Santa Cruz was replaced by a sharply-focused determination.

At 7:00 A.M. HMS *Sirius* on station off Cadiz made the signal, "The enemy's ships are coming out of port." In less than two hours the signal had been relayed by a string of ships positioned for the purpose to Nelson 50 miles away.[99] Immediately Nelson headed for the Combined Fleet, still led by Admiral Villeneuve, and at daylight on October 21 the adversaries were in sight of one another. Now the battle was only hours away.

There's an ironic historical coincidence associated with the commencement of combat off Cape Trafalgar. On that day at Ulm, Napoleon achieved one of his greatest land victories with a crushing defeat of the Austrian army. A French general at the scene, Marshal Marmont, wrote of the victory: "What transports of delight among our soldiers!" The general went on to say, "with that army there was nothing you could not undertake, no enterprise that would not succeed."[100] The contrast of Napoleon's success at Ulm, at the precise time omimous events foreshadowing his future were taking place at Trafalgar, underscores how profoundly Nelson shaped history with his unprecedented exploits at sea.

It's also interesting to note the difference in attitudes between Nelson and Villeneuve, and between the respective fleets, as the battle approached. Nelson had been seeking all-out combat for years. His subordinate admirals, captains, and their crews also were eager for battle. In contrast, Villeneuve believed that he was overmatched, and he appeared to be unnerved by the prospect of meeting Nelson. He sailed from Cadiz only because he knew his relief had been ordered by Napoleon, and he probably faced disgrace upon return to Paris. After the battle Collingwood reported that Villeneuve, who had been captured during the battle, "acknowledges that they cannot contend with us at sea."[101] In addition, there was dissension between the French and Spanish captains, and inevitably these undercurrents had to have affected the crews of the French and Spanish ships.

Approximate Positions at the Beginning of the Battle of Trafalgar

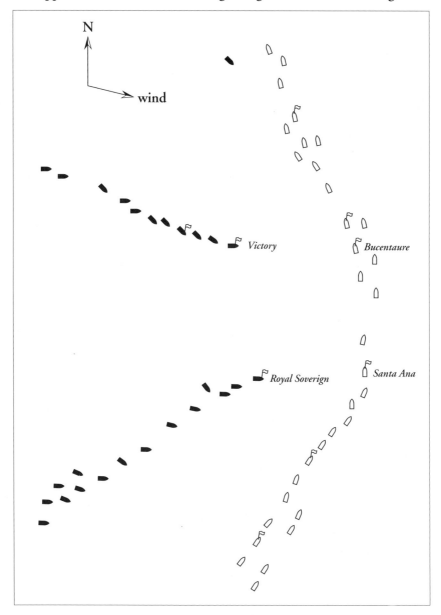

N

wind

Victory

Bucentaure

Royal Soverign

Santa Ana

● British ships (27)   Admirals' flagships
◁ Combined French and Spanish ships (33)

The Battle is Joined

Initially both fleets lacked precise formations, but by late morning the shape of the battle was clearer. Villeneuve with 33 ships-of-the-line had organized his fleet into a traditional but somewhat modified line-ahead. His ships formed a shallow crescent, concave from the point of view of the attacking British. The French line was irregular, with a number of ships sailing side-by-side rather than bow-to-stern. This irregularity actually made Nelson's plan to break through the French line more challenging.

Nelson with 27 ships-of-the-line followed the general intent of his Memorandum of 9 October by attacking the middle and rear of the combined French-Spanish fleet with two divisions—rather than the three described in the Memorandum—sailing roughly parallel courses. During their approach in light winds Nelson's flagship, HMS *Victory*, and Collingwood's, HMS *Royal Sovereign*, were leading their divisions head-on into the combined fleet. In that phase of the battle, the British were exposed for considerable time to the broadsides of the combined fleet, while they were unable to bring more than a few bow guns to bear. However, Nelson's tactic was a means of creating the maximum shock on the enemy line. His attack on Villeneuve's fleet was characterized by quickness and concentration of force. The ultimate tactical objective was to create the eyeball-to-eyeball, smashing combat in which the rapid-file gunnery proficiency of the British would be an advantage.

The weather division led by Nelson, contained 12 ships, including four three-deckers. The lee division led by Collingwood numbered 15 ships, including three three-deckers. As with the French, the British divisions were not perfectly formed, and some witnesses saw them as clusters of ships rather than columns. Around noon Collingwood smashed into the combined fleet at the fifth ship from the rear, the *Santa Ana*, the flagship of Spanish Vice Admiral Alava. The *Royal Sovereign*'s double-shotted, opening broadside raked the stern of the *Santa Ana* with devastating effect, killing or wounding an estimated 400 members of her crew. It was a stunning first blow that established the tenor for what followed.

The division led by Nelson in the *Victory* fell on the middle of the combined fleet about 45 minutes after Collingwood's first blow. As it did so, the *Victory* headed for a cluster of ships just astern of the *Bucentaure*, Admiral Villeneuve's flagship. Nelson entered the fray with a ferocity that matched Collingwood's; the *Victory* fired a 68-pound carronade, charged with one round shot and a keg of 500 musket balls into the stern of Villeneuve's flagship. That was quickly followed by a point-blank broadside from guns that were double or triple shotted. As with Collingwood's first blow, the result was devastating and approximately 400 crewmembers of the *Bucentaure* were killed or wounded. Nelson completed the powerful one-two punch and established the momentum that carried the British to victory.

What followed over several hours was the pell-mell battle Nelson wanted, with scores of individual slugging matches—the equivalent of hand-to-hand combat—among ships. The superior close-range gunnery and discipline of the British were telling. About 5:30 in the afternoon the French *Achille* blew up, ending the day's combat carnage. Although Nelson's ships were badly mauled, none sank or were taken by the combined fleet. In contrast the combined fleet lost the *Achille*, plus 17 ships captured by the British.[102]

The elation of the victory was counterbalanced, however, by the death of Nelson. At about 1:30 P.M. a bullet, presumed to have been fired by a sniper from one of the tops high above the main deck of the French ship *Redoutable*, struck Nelson and severed his backbone. Sometime between 4:30 and 5 P.M. he died, after his last words, "Thank God I have done my duty."[103]

The totality of the victory was jeopardized by a vicious, three-day storm that threatened the destruction of both the British fleet and the prizes it had captured. Nature added the final punctuation to the story of destruction written during the combat. Nelson anticipated the storm before the combat began, and one of his dying instructions to his flag captain was to anchor the moment the battle ended. To the end Nelson demonstrated the seaman's instincts learned as a boy along Norfolk's shores. His instructions to anchor saved many lives and preserved a victory that would have surely been negated by the storm. The result was, as Collingwood put it, "The Combined Fleet is destroyed." [104]

Beyond Doctrine and Tactics

An important aspect of Nelson's leadership demonstrated at Trafalgar was his ability to establish a winning combat doctrine among his subordinates. Before the battle was joined, Nelson made it clear what had to be accomplished and the combat doctrine that should be followed. Linked to that establishment of a winning doctrine was his reliance on the judgment and initiative of his senior officers to react to the battle's unpredictable circumstances. And it all was undergirded by the emotional connection between the fleet and its leader.

As important as were Nelson's ability to establish a winning fighting doctrine and his subordinate's professionalism and motivation, there's another dimension to the Battle of Trafalgar that is significant. Nelson was able to think and lead beyond doctrine and tactics. Officers like Admiral Jervis, who broke the enemy's formation at the Battle of Cape St. Vincent in 1797, and Admiral Duncan, who used two columns to split the Dutch formation at the Battle of Camperdown in the same year, had paved the way tactically. [105] But Nelson brought something extra to his battles, his unique warfighting personality.

It was not a matter—as some contend—of Nelson being a maverick bent on defying Royal Navy doctrine willy-nilly. Contrary to much popular wisdom, the Battle of Trafalgar did not represent a radical departure from the Royal Navy's Fighting Instructions. In fact, those instructions went far beyond maintaining a line-ahead formation in battle, and allowed for considerable latitude by fleet commanders. It was a matter of the Royal Navy's Fighting Instructions and Nelson's brilliant combat leadership adding up to a fighting force that was greater than the sum of its parts. Nelson's personal bravery, recognition of the importance of his admirals and captains, concern for the men in his fleets, and reputation as a combat winner, were compounded into a unique force. That force raised the expectations and performance of those who fought with him and compromised those of his enemies.

In addition to recognizing the special qualities that made Nelson a winner in combat, it's worth reemphasizing the long-term results of his successes. Then Captain A. T. Mahan summed up those results expansively. He wrote: "There were, indeed, consequences momentous and stupendous yet to flow from the decisive supremacy of Great Britain's sea-power, the establishment of which, beyond all question or competition, was Nelson's great achievement."[106]

In the shorter-term view many identified the Battle of Trafalgar as the true beginning of the end for Britain's powerful Continental enemy, Napoleon. While in the longer-term view, as a result of Napoleon's eventual defeat, Britain was able to build the first truly global empire and benefit from the commercial, cultural, and military advantages that went with it.

Nelson forever looks seaward from atop his
dramatic monument—designed by William
Railton—in Trafalgar Square. This is the best
known of Nelson's innumerable monuments.
Its epic proportions and central location in
London are appropriate to the role Nelson
played in the maturation of British sea power.

Epilogue

After two hundred years of historical and military analysis—and biographies beyond counting—does revisiting Horatio Nelson's career have any relevance today? Or is it just a fascinating historical interlude, something overtaken by modern technology and a kinder, gentler society? It would be interesting to get answers to that question from Admiral Nelson himself. Perhaps stretching the imagination to envisage an interview with a modern TV reporter would produce something along the following lines.

Reporter: *Admiral, what was the most important influence on your success in battle?*

Nelson: Many things guided me. The influences of my mother and father were important, but the most important was what I learned from my seniors in the Royal Navy. It was that great fighting captain, William Locker, who taught me uncommon well as a young officer that the best way to beat a Frenchman was to lay him close. And it was Admiral Sir John Jervis who showed me as a fleet commander the meaning of the order to "take, burn, sink, or otherwise destroy all enemy vessels of every description." The fighting spirit and winning tradition of men like Captain Locker and Admiral Jervis, and the many others who came before them, was something I took with me on every occasion I met the enemy. That will to win was an important part of my successes. And you must realize that once that kind of tradition is lost it takes many generations to rebuild it; in fact, once lost it probably can never be regained.

Reporter: *Is that kind of tradition still important today? After all, there's been a lot of progress in using diplomacy and organizations like the United Nations to prevent war.*

Nelson: My answer is that of a plain seaman. If you are going to spend the lives of your military people, you must always fight to win. To do otherwise is criminal. By the way, when I was reading *The Times* of London earlier today, I realized that there is quite a bit of serious strife still going on in the world. There must have been at least a dozen armed conflicts, any one of which could expand into a major war.

Reporter: *Admiral, what do you think about women in combat?*

Nelson: Madam, in combat I never think about women at all! But forgive my poor attempt at humor; I know that question is important these days. You do know of course that there were often women aboard Royal Navy ships in my time, and they frequently fought alongside the men. However it was not a formal arrangement, and it was up to each captain to decide if women were to be carried aboard the ship.

I believe the most important thing is that fighting effectiveness must never be reduced by so much as an inch. And women who understand military matters would, I believe agree. But if the nation wills it, it then must be accomplished in ways that meet that requirement. One thing is certain; if someone from Whitehall had tried to tell me how many, and where in my fleet, women should be placed, my words would have gotten me into a confounded scrape.

Reporter: *Sir, has advanced technology changed the kind of leaders needed in modern combat?*

Nelson: Never in life madam. It would seem to me that the basic requirements are the same. It still takes a certain amount of physical courage. But it is the intangible that is most important. I've seen many people in battle, and the leaders who win in combat have an extra dimension—a quality that begins with the willingness to risk life and career to go for a clear victory. It's something that sets them apart when the fighting gets warm.

That's why I felt so strongly about my captains, my Band of Brothers. I knew they would never hesitate in the face of danger, and that they would make good decisions. That last part is particularly important, you know. A good battle plan can take you only so far. Once the event starts, decisions must be made in an instant, on the spot, and in rapidly changing circumstances, and they have to be made in the midst of terrible violence. Those decisions can not be written into a plan, and they cannot be made by someone who is distant from the scene. It is on those decisions that the outcome of the battle ultimately rests.

Reporter: *But with the modern means of communication and electronic displays, why can't the decisions in battle be made by someone at a distance from the confusion of combat?*

Nelson: In battle, there are too many things that can never be predicted. Weather, equipment failure, unexpected capability on the part of the enemy are just a few unpredictable factors. Naval officers traditionally have been selected and trained to make decisions based on the situation as it develops on the scene of battle. It is nonsensical to think battles can be successfully led by remote control.

Reporter: *Do you ever think back to some of your battles?*

Nelson: A few days past I was having a bit of cheese and English beer with my friend Antonio, General Gutiérrez, and we were discussing our battle at Santa Cruz. He asked me my opinion about why I suffered such a decisive defeat at the hands of his troops. I explained that the most important factor was combat leadership. It wasn't that we did not have good ships and men. His Lordship, Admiral Jervis, provided my squadron with some of his best ships, and the men fought like the devil.

Some people say we had bad luck with the wind and weather, but we could have overcome those early problems. It was mostly a matter of underestimating the ability and determination of my adversary, the General. So, you see, I learned something from that battle besides how to write with my left hand.

Reporter: *Admiral, how can a country be sure to have leaders who will win in battle?*

Nelson: Government and the military must encourage the people who show the right qualities, boldness for example. The problem is that sometimes the people who show some of the signs of being good combat leaders are not very popular. Often they make civilians nervous. And political leaders say foolish things like "people who train to fight wars are out of touch with society." I can only say that preparing yourself to fight in battle does tend to focus your attention more narrowly than if you are, say, a tradesman preparing to open your shop for business. But that intense focus is a sign of a personality that will win for your country in battle.

I have to add that there is no guarantee of victory. Admiral Jervis wrote to me before the Battle of Santa Cruz that mortals cannot command victory, they can only deserve it. By deserving it, I believe he meant doing everything possible to win, including fostering the best combat leadership as a steady policy.

Reporter: *Who is your favorite naval leader since your time?*

Nelson: I admire Arleigh Burke very much. When he was a ship captain and a destroyer squadron commander during World War II, he was very aggressive. He was the one who said that the difference between a good officer and a great officer is about ten seconds. He also fought hard for what he thought was right when he was a senior officer in your Pentagon. Once he decided that something was the right thing to do, he just kept at it. That was courage, too.

Reporter: *Are the lessons learned from your career of any importance beyond the Royal Navy?*

Nelson: I would remind you that many of the traditions in the American Navy were carried over from the Royal Navy. Yes, you did do some things differently in the Colonial Navy, but there was a lot of carryover too. Think about this: the words "I have not yet begun to fight" expressed, quite well as a matter of fact, the exact reaction I had at the Battle of Copenhagen when I was ordered to withdraw. I think it is more than coincidence that there continues to be a special relationship between the Royal Navy and the U.S. Navy today. Standards of conduct and performance under fire cannot be established overnight. On the other hand, those standards can be destroyed quickly when, as I once wrote to Lady Hamilton, "Government don't care much for us."

Reporter: *Sir, a lot of people say you compromised your career by your repeated refusal of orders from Admiral Lord Keith while you were in command in the Mediterranean in 1799. What do you say to that?*

Nelson: I say, a lot of people were not there at the time.

Reporter: *Why were you able to defeat the French naval forces so consistently and, in the process, prevent Napoleon from achieving French hegemony in Europe?*

Nelson: There are at least two different reasons. First Napoleon never had confidence in his navy. He did not understand how to use his naval power, so it was not surprising his fleets did not meet their full potential in battle. Second, the French government drove many of its best naval officers out of the service during the French Revolution because of the political incorrectness of those officers. As a result Napoleon did not have the benefit of the best available naval combat leadership, and this was quite evident in battle. There is a strong lesson in those circumstances because, in fact, the French ships were in some ways superior to our own, and they frequently outnumbered us in battle.

Reporter: *Admiral Nelson, is there anything else you would like to say to the audience before we finish this interview?*

Nelson: Yes, I'd like to repeat for your audience something I wrote to the Right Honorable Henry Addington in 1803: Prevention is better than cure.

Endnotes

Chapter 1

1. For examples of the U.S. Navy's attention to the subject see the former Naval Doctrine Command's studies: *Navy Combat Leadership for Tomorrow: Where Will We Get Such Men and Women?* by Dr. James J. Tritten, July 1995, and *A Charismatic Dimension of Military Leadership?* by Dr. James J. Tritten and Dr. David M. Keithly, May 1995.

2. "The Military Must Revive Its Warrior Spirit," William C. Moore, *The Wall Street Journal*, 10/27/98, A22.

3. Geoffrey Bennett, *Nelson the Commander*, Charles Scribner's Sons, New York City, 1972, Foreword.

4. A. T. Mahan, *The Life of Nelson*, Little, Brown, and Company, Boston, 1897, Preface.

Chapter 3

5. *The Dispatches and Letters of Lord Nelson*, Vol. I, edited by Sir Nicholas Harris Nicolas, Henry Colburn, London 1844; republished by Chatham Publishing, London, 1998, 329.

6. Tom Pocock, *Nelson and His World*, Book Club Associates, London, 1974, 5.

7. *The Dispatches and Letters of Lord Nelson*, Vol. VII, edited by Sir Nicholas Harris Nicolas, Henry Colburn, London, 1846; republished by Chatham Publishing, London, 1998, 139.

8. Robert Southey, *The Life of Nelson*, Vol. I, John Murray, London, 1813, 5 (also published in numerous later additions).

9. *The Dispatches and Letters of Lord Nelson*, Vol. V, edited by Sir Nicholas Harris Nicolas, Henry Colburn, London, 1845; republished by Chatham Publishing, London 1998, 254.

10. Robert Southey, *The Life of Nelson*, Vol. II, John Murray, London, 1813, 186.

11. *The Dispatches and Letters of Lord Nelson*, Vol. III, edited by Sir Nicholas Harris Nicolas, Henry Colburn, London, 1845; republished by Chatham Publishing, London, 1998, 355.

Chapter 4

12. *Dictionary of Military and Naval Quotations*, edited by Robert Debs Heinl, Jr. (quote from "War As I Knew It," 1947), United States Naval Institute Press, 1966, 220.

13. *The Dispatches and Letters of Lord Nelson*, Vol. IV, edited by Sir Nicholas Harris Nicolas, Henry Colburn, London, 1845; republished by Chatham Publishing, London, 1998, 284.

14. Colin White, *1797 Nelson's Year of Destiny*, the Royal Naval Museum, Portsmouth/Sutton Publishing Limited, Gloucestershire, 1998, 58.

15. Tom Pocock, *Horatio Nelson*, The Bodley Head, London, Third Edition 1988, 20.

16. *The Nelson Touch*, compiled by Clemence Dane, William Heinemann Ltd., London and Toronto, 1942, 88.

17. *The Dispatches and Letters of Lord Nelson*, Vol. IV, edited by Sir Nicholas Harris Nicolas, by Henry Colburn, London, 1845; republished by Chatham Publishing, London, 1998, 309.

18. Ibid., Vol. VII, edited by Sir Nicholas Harris Nicolas, Henry Colburn, London, 1846; republished by Chatham Publishing, London, 1998, 33.

19. Ibid., Vol. V, 414.

20. Ibid. Vol. V, 238.

21. The Nelson Collection at Lloyd's is described in detail in *The Nelson Collection at Lloyd's*, edited by Warren R. Dawson, published by Macmillan & Co. Limited, London, and in a brief brochure published by Lloyd's.

22. Carola Oman, *Nelson*, The Reprint Society, London, 1950 (first published by Hodder and Stoughton Ltd., 1947), 566.

Chapter 5

23. *The Dispatches and Letters of Lord Nelson*, Vol. I, edited by Nicholas Harris Nicolas, Henry Colburn, London, 1844; republished by Chatham Publishing, London, 1998, 133.

24. Ibid. Vol. II, 2.

25. Roger Morriss, *Nelson: The Life and Letters of a Hero*, Collins & Brown Limited, London, 1996, 49.

26. *The Dispatches and Letters of Lord Nelson*, Vol. I, edited by Nicholas Harris Nicolas, Henry Colburn, London, 1844; republished by Chatham Publishing, London, 1998, 150.

27. Ibid., 216.

28. *Nelson's Letters to His Wife and Other Documents*, edited by George P. B. Naish, Routledge & Kegan Paul Ltd., London, in conjunction with the Naval Records Society, 1958, 350.

29. *The Dispatches and Letters of Lord Nelson*, Vol. I, edited by Nicholas Harris Nicolas, Henry Colburn, London, 1844; republished by Chatham Publishing, London, 1998, 326.

30. Ibid., Vol. VII, 40.

31. Ibid., Vol. IV, 284.

32. Clemence Dane, *The Nelson Touch: An Anthology of Lord Nelson's Letters*, William Heinemann Ltd., London, 1942, 150.

Chapter 6

33. *The Dispatches and Letters of Lord Nelson*, Vol. I, edited by Sir Nicholas Harris Nicolas, Henry Colburn, London, 1844, 116.

34. Ibid., 129.

35. Ibid., 167.

36. Ibid. Vol. II, 436.

37. Ibid. Vol. VI, 427.

38. Ibid. Vol. VII, 35.

39. Ibid., 56.

40. The signal that Nelson ordered initially was "England confides that, etc." The word "expects" was substituted for "confides" because it was easier to construct with the Royal Navy flag signal system of the day.

Chapter 7

41. Roger Morriss, *Nelson: The Life and Letters of a Hero*, Collins & Brown Limited, London, 1996, 105.

42. Ibid., 106.

43. *The Dispatches and Letters of Lord Nelson*, Vol II, edited by Sir Nicholas Harris Nicolas, Henry Colburn, London, 1845; republished by Chatham Publishing, London, 1998, 434–5.

44. Tom Pocock, *Nelson and his world*, Book Club Associates, London, 1947, 126.

45. Tom Pocock, *Horatio Nelson*, The Bodley Head third reprint, London, 1988, 309.

46. A. T. Mahan, *The Life of Nelson*, Little, Brown, and Company, Boston, 1899 (second edition), IX of Preface.

47. *Nelson against Napoleon*, edited by Robert Gardiner, Chatham Publishing, London/Naval Institute Press, Annapolis, 1997, 11.

48. *Nelson's Letters to His Wife and Other Documents*, edited by George P. B. Naish, Routledge & Kegan Paul Ltd., London, in conjunction with the Naval Records Society, 1958, 596.

49. David Howarth and Stephen Howarth, *Nelson: The Immortal Memory*, J. M. Dent & Sons Ltd., London, 1988, 2.

50. Tom Pocock, *Nelson and his world*, Book Club Associates, London, 1947, 70.

51. *Nelson: An Illustrated History*, edited by Pieter van der Merwe, Laurence King Publishing in association with the National Maritime Museum, 1995, 136.

52. Carola Oman, *Nelson*, The Reprint Society, London, 1950, 552.

53. *The Dispatches and Letters of Lord Nelson*, Vol. II, edited by Sir Nicholas Harris Nicolas, Henry Colburn, London, 1845; republished by Chatham Publishing, London, 1998, 340.

54. Ibid., 346.

55. Ibid. Vol. IV, 309.

56. This prayer can be found in many works about Nelson and is affixed to his sarcophagus in St. Paul's Cathedral, London.

57. *Nelson: An Illustrated History*, edited by Pieter van der Merwe, Laurence King in Association with the National Maritime Museum, 1995, 109.

Chapter 8

58. Nicolas Tracy, *Nelson's Battles: The Art of Victory in the Age of Sail*, Chatham Publishing, London/Naval Institute Press, Annapolis, 1996, 94.

59. Colin White, *1797 Nelson's Year of Destiny*, Sutton Publishing Limited, Gloucestershire/Royal Naval Museum, Portsmouth, 1998, 55–71.

60. *The Dispatches and Letters of Lord Nelson*, Vol. II, edited by Nicholas Harris Nicolas, Henry Colburn, London, 1845, republished by Chatham Publishing, London, 1998, 337.

61. G. L. Newnham Collingwood, *A Selection from the Public and Private Correspondence of Vice-Admiral Lord Collingwood*, G. & C. & H. Carvill, New York City, 1829 (from the fourth London edition), 42.

Chapter 9

62. *The Dispatches and Letters of Lord Nelson*, Vol. II, edited by Nicholas Harris Nicolas, Henry Colburn, London, 1845; republished by Chatham Publishing, London, 1998, 379–80.

63. Clennell Wilkinson, *Nelson*, George G. Harrap & Co. Ltd., London, Bombay, Sydney, 1931,129.

64. *The Dispatches and Letters of Lord Nelson*, Vol. II, edited by Sir Nicholas Harris Nicolas, Henry Colburn, London, 1846; republished by Chatham Publishing, London, 1998, 413.

65. Ibid., 425

66. Colin White, *1797 Nelson's Year of Destiny*, the Royal Naval Museum, Portsmouth/Sutton Publishing Ltd., Gloucestershire, 1998, 115.

67. *The Dispatches and Letters of Lord Nelson*, Vol. VII, edited by Sir Nicholas Harris Nicolas, Henry Colburn, London, 1846; republished by Chatham Publishing, London, 1998, ccxxi of Additional Letters.

68. Ernle Bradford, *Nelson the Essential Hero*, Harcourt Brace Jovanovich, New York and London, 1997, 155.

69. Printed description of the aftermath of the battle provided by the Museo Militar, Santa Cruz, Tenerife, Canary Islands.

70. *Nelson's Letters to His Wife and Other Documents*, edited by George P. B. Naish, Routledge & Kegan Paul Ltd., London, in conjunction with the Naval Records Society, 1958, 374.

71. *The Dispatches and Letters of Lord Nelson*, Vol. II, edited by Sir Nicholas Harris Nicolas, Henry Colburn, London, 1845; republished by Chatham Publishing, London, 1998, 434.

72. Ibid., 435.

73. Colin White, *1797 Nelson's Year of Destiny*, the Royal Naval Museum, Portsmouth/Sutton Publishing Ltd., Gloucestershire, 1998, 101.

Chapter 10

74. For an analysis of events leading up to the Battle of the Nile and the Battle, see *Nelson against Napoleon*, edited by Robert Gardiner, Chatham Publishing, London/Naval Institute Press, Annapolis, 1997, 9–36.

75. *The Dispatches and Letters of Lord Nelson*, Vol. III, edited by Sir Nicholas Harris Nicolas, Henry Colburn, London, 1845; republished by Chatham Publishing, London, 1998, 17.

76. *Nelson against Napoleon*, edited by Robert Gardiner, Chatham Publishing, London/Naval Institute Press, Annapolis, 1997, 28.

77. *The Dispatches and Letters of Lord Nelson*, Vol. III, edited by Sir Nicholas Harris Nicolas, Henry Colburn, London, 1845; republished by Chatham Publishing, London, 1998, 48.

78. Ibid., 98.

79. Ibid., 56.

80. Tom Pocock, *Horatio Nelson*, The Bodley Head, London, third reprint 1988, 168.

81. Oliver Warner, *The Battle of the Nile*, B. T. Batsford, London, 1960, 137.

82. *The Dispatches and Letters of Lord Nelson*, Vol. III, edited by Sir Nicholas Harris Nicolas, Henry Colburn, London, 1845; republished by Chatham Publishing, 1998, 72.

83. Ibid., 83.

Chapter 11

84. Nicholas Tracy, *Nelson's Battles: The Art of Victory in the Age of Sail*, Chatham Publishing, London/Naval Institute Press, Annapolis, 1996, 133.

85. *The Dispatches and Letters of Lord Nelson*, Vol. IV, edited by Sir Nicholas Harris Nicolas, Henry Colburn, London, 1845; republished by Chatham Publishing, London, 1998, 294.

86. Ibid., 360.

87. Dudley Pope, *The Great Gamble: Nelson at Copenhagen*, Simon and Schuster, New York, 1972, 499.

Chapter 12

88. Oliver Warner, *Trafalgar*, B. T. Batsford Ltd., London, 1959, 158.

89. Dudley Pope, *Decision at Trafalgar*, J. B. Lippincott Company, Philadelphia & New York, 1959, 11.

90. John Terraine, *Trafalgar*, Wordsworth Editions Limited (Wordsworth Military Library), Hertfordshire, 1998, back cover.

91. Roger Morriss, *The Campaign of Trafalgar*, edited by Robert Gardiner, Chatham Publishing, London, 1997, 10.

92. Ibid., 10.

93. *The Dispatches and Letters of Lord Nelson*, Vol. VI, edited by Sir Nicholas Harris Nicolas, Henry Colburn, London, 1846; republished by Chatham Publishing, London, 1998, 253.

94. Ibid., 125.

95. *The Dispatches and Letters of Lord Nelson*, Vol. VII, edited by Sir Nicholas Harris Nicolas, Henry Colburn, London, 1846; republished by Chatham Publishing, London, 1998, 80.

96. Ibid., 66.

97. Roger Morriss, *The Campaign at Trafalgar*, (edited by Robert Gardiner), Chatham Publishing, London 1997, 130.

98. *The Dispatches and Letters of Lord Nelson*, Vol. VII, edited by Sir Nicholas Harris Nicolas, Henry Colburn, London, 1846; republished by Chatham Publishing, London, 1998, 89.

99. John Terraine, *Trafalgar*, Wordsworth Editions Limited (Wordsworth Military Library), Hertfordshire, 1998, 134.

100. Ibid., 127.

101. *The Dispatches and Letters of Lord Nelson*, Vol. VII, edited by Sir Nicholas Harris Nicolas, Henry Colburn, London, 1846; republished by Chatham Publishing, London, 1998, 236.

102. Nicholas Tracy, *Nelson's Battles*, Naval Institute Press, Annapolis, 1996, 199.

103. For a description of the Battle of Trafalgar and Nelson's death, see *The Dispatches and Letters of Lord Nelson*, Vol. VII, edited by Sir Nicholas Harris Nicolas, Henry Colburn, London, 1846; republished by Chatham Publishing, London, 1998, beginning 142.

104. Ibid., 233.

105. James J. Tritten, *Doctrine and Fleet Tactics in the Royal Navy*, U.S. Naval Doctrine Command Report, November 1994.

106. A. T. Mahan, *The Life of Nelson*, Little, Brown, and Company, Boston, Second Edition, 1899, 742.

Bibliography

The following works are among the best references on Nelson. The list is by no means all-inclusive. If you are interested in further reading on Nelson, consult the bibliographies in *The Nelson Companion* and *Nelson: An Illustrated History*, listed below. Both of these books contain excellent bibliographies, although they do not include books published since 1995.

Special References

The Dispatches and Letters of Lord Nelson, edited by Nicholas Harris Nicolas, Henry Colburn, London, seven volumes published between 1844–46 and republished in 1998 by Chatham Publishing, London.

Nelson's Letters to His Wife and Other Documents, edited by George P. B. Naish, Routledge & Kegan Paul Ltd. In conjunction with the Navy Records Society, London, 1958.

Nelson: An Illustrated History, edited by Pieter van der Merwe, Laurence King Publishing, London, 1995.

The Nelson Companion, edited by Colin White, Alan Sutton Publishing Ltd., Gloucestershire/Naval Institute Press, Annapolis, 1995.

Biography

The Life of Admiral Lord Nelson, Clarke and M'Arthur, T. Cadwell and W. Davis in the Strand, London, 1809.

Memoirs of the Life of Vice-Admiral Lord Viscount Nelson, Thomas Joseph Pettigrew, T. and W. Boone, London, 1849.

The Life of Nelson, Robert Southey, John Murray, London, 1813 (this biography has been reprinted many times, including several recent editions).

The Life of Nelson, A. T. Mahan, Little, Brown and Company, Boston, 1897.

Nelson, Carola Oman, Hodder & Stoughton Ltd., London, 1947.

Nelson the Commander, Geoffrey Bennett, Charles Scribner's Sons, New York, 1972.

Nelson the Essential Hero, Ernle Bradford, Harcourt Brace Jovanovich, New York and London, 1977.

Horatio Nelson, Tom Pocock, The Bodley Head, London, 1988.

Nelson: The Immortal Memory, David and Stephen Howarth, J. M. Dent & Sons Ltd., London, 1988.

Nelson: The Life and Letters of a Hero, Roger Morriss, Collins & Brown in Association with the National Maritime Museum, London, 1996.

Particular Contexts

Nelson Against Napoleon, edited by Robert Gardiner, Chatham Publishing, London/Naval Institute Press, Annapolis, 1997.

Nelson's Navy, Brian Lavery, Conway Maritime Press Ltd., London/Naval Institute Press, Annapolis, 1989.

1797: Nelson's Year of Destiny, Colin White, Royal Naval Museum, Portsmouth/Sutton Publishing Limited, Gloucestershire, 1998.

Men-of-War: Life in Nelson's Navy, Patrick O'Brian, W. W. Norton & Company (American Edition), New York, 1995.

Battles

Sea Battles in Close-up: The Age of Nelson, David Lyon, Ian Allan Publishing, Surrey/Naval Institute Press, Annapolis, 1996.

Nelson's Battles, Oliver Warner, B. T. Batsford Ltd., London, 1965.

Nelson's Battles: The Art of Victory in the Age of Sail, Nicholas Tracy, Chatham Publishing, London/Naval Institute Press, Annapolis, 1996.

The Battle of the Nile, Oliver Warner, B. T. Batsford Ltd., London, 1961.

The Great Gamble-Nelson at Copenhagen, Dudley Pope, Simon and Schuster, New York, 1972.

The Campaign of Trafalgar: 1803–1805, edited by Robert Gardiner, Chatham Publishing, London/Naval Institute Press, Annapolis, 1997.

The Campaign of Trafalgar, J. S. Corbett, Longmans, Green & Co., London, 1910.

Decision at Trafalgar, Dudley Pope, J. B. Lippincott Company, Philadelphia, 1960.

The Trafalgar Roll: The Ships and Officers, Robert Holden Mackenzie, Lionell Leventhal Limited, London/Naval Institute Press, Annapolis, 1989.

Trafalgar and the Spanish Navy, John D. Harbron, Conway Maritime Press Ltd., London, 1988.

Others

The Nelson Collection at Lloyd's, Warren R. Dawson, Macmillan & Co., 1932.

The 100-Gun Ship Victory, John McKay, Conway Maritime Press Ltd., London/Naval Institute Press, Annapolis, 1987.

Sea Life in Nelson's Time, John Masefield, Conway Maritime Press, London, 1984.

Nelson's Last Diary, a facsimile edited by Oliver Warner, The Kent State Press, Kent State University, Ohio/Seeley, Service & Co. Ltd., London, 1971.

Acknowledgments

I want to acknowledge the editors and staff members at the U.S. Naval Institute and the National Maritime Historical Society who—since I decided to write fulltime—have provided much needed encouragement and guidance to me.

Additional recognition is due the Australian National Maritime Museum in Sydney, the Royal Naval Museum in Portsmouth, and the Royal Navy. Their cooperation, plus the kind permission of the Dean and Chapter, St. Paul's Cathedral, London, made it possible for me to take most of the photos that are included in this book.

I am also indebted to this book's editor and designer, C. C. Dickinson, who with steadfast professionalism and insight has contributed mightily to whatever is good in these pages and to the cover's designer, Steven Burns, for his eye-catching design.

Finally, I thank that special group of Britons who with patient good humor continue to assist my efforts to understand the true character of their Admiral Lord Nelson.

Index

C

Ça Ira, 62

Cadiz, 10, 12, 21, 80, 99, 101, 104–106

Calder, Sir Robert, 62–63, 66, 104

Calvi, 10, 15, 32

Camperdown, Battle of, 110

Cape St. Vincent, Battle of, 10, 16, 22, 28, 32, 43–45, 56, 61–68, 110

Capriai, 71

Captain, HMS, 10, 56, 62

Caracciolo, Admiral, 10, 20

Carcass, HMS, 21

Catherine, Nelson's mother, 8, 25

character, defined by writers and philosophers, 19

character, related to combat leadership, 19–28

Chesapeake Bay, x

Collingwood, Vice Admiral, 55, 63, 105–106, 108–110

combined fleet, 106, 108–109

concern for the common seamen, connection with combat leadership, 27

Copenhagen, 11, 16, 22–23, 27, 45, 51, 57–58, 89–98, 103, 117

Corfu, 87

Cornwallis, Admiral Sir William, 58

Cornwallis, General, x

Correglia, Adelaide, 29

Corsican naval campaign, 10, 32

Culloden, HMS, 63, 71–72, 84

D

Davison, Alexander, 45–46, 92

de Córdoba, Admiral, 62

DeGrasse, Admiral, x

Dey of Algiers, 101

doctrine and character, link between, 20

Dolphin, HMS, 23

Drake, 45, 61, 70

Drinkwater, Colonel John, 67

duty, defined by Nelson, 24, 26, 37, 39–47, 57

E

East India Company, 26

Elephant, HMS, 94–96

Elliot, Sir Gilbert, 67

Emerald, HMS, 71–72

Engage the Enemy More Closely, flag signal, 83

England Expects That Every Man Will Do His Duty, flag signal, 46

F

Fighting Instructions, of the Royal Navy, 110

Fitzgerald, F. Scott, 19

flag signals, famous, 46, 83, 98

Foley, Captain, 84–85

Fox, HMS, 55, 71–72, 75

Frederick, Crown Prince, 93

G

Gardiner, Robert, 81

Goethe, 19

Goliath, HMS, 84–85

Greville, Charles, 33–34

Gutiérrez, General Antonio, 72–74, 76–78, 116

H

Hamilton, Emma Lady, 6, 10–15, 17, 21, 29, 33–38, 43, 48, 50, 54, 105

Hamilton, Sir William, 10, 33

Hawkins, 70

Herbert, John, 30–31

WELCOME TO

Hellgate Press

Hellgate Press is named after the historic and rugged Hellgate Canyon on southern Oregon's scenic Rogue River. The raging river that flows below the canyon's towering jagged cliffs has always attracted a special sort of individual — someone who seeks adventure. From the pioneers who bravely pursued the lush valleys beyond, to the anglers and rafters who take on its roaring challenges today — Hellgate Press publishes books that personify this adventurous spirit. Our books are about military history, adventure travel, and outdoor recreation. On the following pages, we would like to introduce you to some of our latest titles and encourage you to join in the celebration of this unique spirit.

Our books are in your favorite bookstore or
you can order them direct at **1-800-228-2275**
or visit our Website at **http://www.psi-research.com**

ARMY MUSEUMS

West of the Mississippi   ISBN: 1-55571-395-5
by Fred L. Bell, SFC Retired   Paperback: 17.95

A guide book for travelers to the army museums of the west, as well as a source of information about the history of the site where the museum is located. Contains detailed information about the contents of the museum and interesting information about famous soldiers stationed at the location or specific events associated with the facility. These twenty-three museums are in forts and military reservations which represent the colorful heritage in the settling of the American West.

BYRON'S WAR

I Never Will Be Young Again...   ISBN: 1-55571-402-1
by Byron Lane   Hardcover: 21.95

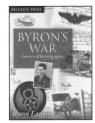

Based on letters that were mailed home and a personal journal written more than fifty years ago during World War II, *Byron's War* brings the war life through the eyes of a very young air crew officer. It depicts how the life of this young American changed through cadet training, the experiences as a crew member flying across the North Atlantic under wartime hazards to the awesome responsibility assigned to a nineteen year-old when leading hundreds of men and aircraft where success or failure could seriously impact the outcome of the war.

GULF WAR DEBRIEFING BOOK
An After Action Report   ISBN: 1-55571-396-3
by Andrew Leyden   Paperback: 18.95

Whereas most books on the Persian Gulf War tell an "inside story" based on someone else's opinion, this book lets you draw your own conclusions by providing you with a meticulous review of events and documentation all at your fingertips. Includes lists of all military units deployed, a detailed account of the primary weapons used during the war, and a look at the people and politics behind the military maneuvering.

FROM HIROSHIMA WITH LOVE
by Raymond A. Higgins   ISBN: 1-55571-404-8
                                          Paperback: 18.95

This remarkable story is written from actual detailed notes and diary entries kept by Lieutenant Commander Wallace Higgins. Because of his industrial experience back in the United States and with the reserve commission in the Navy, he was an excellent choice for military governor of Hiroshima. Higgins was responsible for helping rebuild a ravaged nation of war. He developed an unforeseen respect for the Japanese, the culture, and one special woman.

NIGHT LANDING
A Short History of West Coast Smuggling   ISBN: 1-55571-449-8
by David W. Heron   Paperback: 13.95

Night Landing reveals the true stories of smuggling off the shores of California from the early 1800s to the present. It is a provocative account of the many attempts to illegally trade items such as freon, drugs, sea otters, and diamonds. This unusual chronicle also profiles each of these ingenious, but over-optimistic criminals and their eventual apprehension.

PILOTS, MAN YOUR PLANES!
A History of Naval Aviation   ISBN: 1-55571- 466-8
by Wilbur H. Morrison   Hardbound: 33.95

An account of naval aviation from Kitty Hawk to the Gulf War, *Pilots, Man Your Planes! — A History of Naval Aviation* tells the story of naval air growth from a time when planes were launched from battleships to the major strategic element of naval warfare it is today. Full of detailed maps and photographs. Great for anyone with an interest in aviation.

REBIRTH OF FREEDOM
From Nazis and Communists to a New Life in America
by Michael Sumichrast

ISBN: 1-55571-492-7
Paperback: 16.95

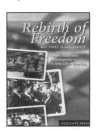

"...a fascinating account of how the skill, ingenuity and work ethics of an individual, when freed from the yoke of tyranny and oppression, can make a lasting contribution to Western society. Michael Sumichrast's autobiography tells of his first loss of freedom to the Nazis, only to have his native country subjected to the tyranny of the Communists. He shares his experiences of life in a manner that makes us Americans, and others, thankful to live in a country where individual freedom is protected."

— *General Alexander M. Haig, Former Secretary of State*

THE WAR THAT WOULD NOT END
U.S. Marines in Vietnam, 1971-1973
by Major Charles D. Melson, USMC (Ret)

ISBN: 1-55571-420-X
Paperback: 19.95

When South Vietnamese troops proved unable to "take over" the war from their American counterparts, the Marines had to resume responsibility. Covering the period 1971-1973, Major Charles D. Melson, who served in Vietnam, describes all the strategies, battles, and units that broke a huge 1972 enemy offensive. The book contains a detailed look at this often ignored period of America's longest war.

WORDS OF WAR
From Antiquity to Modern Times
by Gerald Weland

ISBN: 1-55571-491-9
Paperback: 13.95

Words of War is a delightful romp through military history. Lively writing leads the reader to an under- standing of a number of soldierly quotes. The result of years of haunting dusty dungeons in libraries, obscure journals and microfilm files, this unique approach promises to inspire many casual readers to delve further into the circumstances surrounding the birth of many quoted words.

WORLD TRAVEL GUIDE
by Barry Mowell

ISBN: 1-55571- 494-3
Paperback: 19.95

The resource for the modern traveler, *World Travel Guide* is both informative and enlightening. It contains maps, social and economic information, information concerning entry requirements, availability of healthcare, transportation and crime. Numerous Website and embassy listings are provided. A one-page summary contains general references to the history, culture and other characteristics of interest to the traveler.

K-9 SOLDIERS

Vietnam and After   ISBN: 1-55571-495-1
by Paul B. Morgan   Paperback: 13.95

A retired US Army officer, former Green Beret, Customs K-9 and
Security Specialist, Paul B. Morgan has written *K-9 Soldiers*. In his
book, Morgan relates twenty-four brave stories from his lifetime of
working with man's best friend in combat and on the streets. They
are the stories of dogs and their handlers who work behind the
scenes when a disaster strikes, a child is lost or some bad guy tries
to outrun the cops.

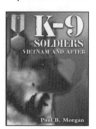

OH, WHAT A LOVELY WAR

A Soldier's Memoir   ISBN: 1-55571-502-8
by Stanley Swift   Paperback: 14.95

This book tells you what history books do not. It is war with a human
face. It is the unforgettable memoir of British soldier Gunner Stanley
Swift through five years of war. Intensely personal and moving, it
documents the innermost thoughts and feelings of a young man as
he moves from civilian to battle-hardened warrior under the duress
of fire.

THROUGH MY EYES

91st Infantry Division, Italian Campaign 1942-1945   ISBN: 1-55571-497-8
by Leon Weckstein   Paperback: 14.95

Through My Eyes is the true account of an Average Joe's infantry days
before, during and shortly after the furiously fought battle for Italy.
The author's front row seat allows him to report the shocking account
of casualties and the rest-time shenanigans during the six weeks of
the occupation of the city of Trieste. He also recounts in detail his
personal roll in saving the historic Leaning Tower of Pisa.

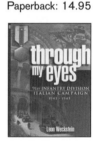

MILITARY HISTORY ADVENTURE

Hellgate Press

1-800-228-2275
or visit our Website at **http://www.psi-research.com**
